Referral in Pastoral Counseling

Referral in Pastoral Counseling

Wm. B. Oglesby, Jr.

Abingdon
Nashville

REFERRAL IN PASTORAL COUNSELING, REVISED EDITION

Copyright © 1968 by Prentice-Hall, Inc.
Copyright © 1978 by William B. Oglesby, Jr.

Library of Congress Cataloging in Publication Data

OGLESBY, WILLIAM B.
  Referral in pastoral counseling.
  Includes index.
  1.   Pastoral counseling.   I.   Title.
  BV4012.2.035   1978   253.5   78-7976

ISBN 0-687-35887-6

MANUFACTURED BY THE PARTHENON PRESS AT
NASHVILLE, TENNESSEE, UNITED STATES OF AMERICA

To those in the great helping professions who have dedicated their lives to the relief of human suffering.

Acknowledgments

It is, of course, impossible to thank all of the persons who have helped to make this book possible. I think of ministers and theological students whose participation in seminar discussions has enriched my own understanding in the search for more effective means of helping. I think of parishioners whom I have known whose cry for help gives tangible meaning to the search. All of these are, properly, not named in this volume; even so, my gratitude to them is nonetheless real.

In addition to the persons whose experiences have provided the substance of the book, I wish to thank Mrs. Evelyn McKittrick for tireless work in typing and correcting the manuscript, and John Brothers for timely assistance in preparing the index. Their help was invaluable in bringing the work to completion.

Wm. B. Oglesby, Jr.
Richmond, Virginia
Winter, 1967

Preface

In the years following the close of World War II, one of the most significant factors in the life of the Church has been the emergence of the minister as a resource for persons experiencing difficulty. While it would be obviously incorrect to imply that prior to this time there was no effective pastoral care, it is evident that today far more people turn to the minister in time of trouble; and indications are that this number is steadily increasing. Every minister can document the statement that requests for his help are not only more numerous, but also more varied as he finds himself involved in the tangled lives of his parishioners as well as of those who have no overt relationship to the Church.

From the standpoint of the minister, this condition presents both opportunity and difficulty. The opportunity lies in the doors that are opened into the lives of all sorts and conditions of men—opportunity to bring the resources of the Gospel to bear on the day-to-day problems that beset all people, to demonstrate that faith is concerned not only with "then and there," but specifically with "here and now." This is an opportunity welcomed by ministers who otherwise might tend to feel that what they say and do appears irrelevant to the average person caught up in the struggles of living.

The difficulty, however, is no less real than the opportunity. It is one thing to have access to the life of another, to be sought after for help, and to be invited into the private distresses which bid fair to overwhelm; but it is another thing to be able to provide the kind of help that is genuine, that truly meets the person where he is, that is effective in enabling the person to meet whatever situation confronts him. One way to put the nature of the difficulty is in the blunt yet realistic words of an old truism. Whenever an individual approaches another for help with the statement, "I have a problem," the immediate inner feeling of the person approached is, "Now, I have a problem! What am I going to do with you? Or for you? Or to you?" However crass this formula, it is certain that it carries the germ of truth which can be recognized by anyone who has been sought out for help.

It should be said at the very outset that both the opportunity and the difficulty must be taken quite seriously. To overlook the opportunity is to belie the very nature of the Gospel. But to minimize the difficulty is to deal superficially with life and death, and to place in jeopardy the future of those whose past has already become twisted in the strain of living.

What, then, is the minister to do? To such a question there can be no absolute answer; but there are guidelines which are of value. First in importance is an accurate assessment of his own resources and skills in dealing with the distresses of life. By the very nature of things, such a task is never-ending. Formal training, increased experience, and continued study and reflection make for a steady expansion of the minister's ability to be of genuine help in time of trouble. While it is true that mere passage of time does not automatically provide greater resourcefulness, it is certain that only time can bring the maturity which is needed to meet the increased burdens of life. Hopefully, every minister should be able to look back and realize that he is far more able to perform the pastoral functions required of him today than he was five years ago.

The second general guideline which is of value in answering the question is the minister's knowledge of the resources available to him and to his parishioners in the other helping professions. As he assesses his own resources, he sees the need for joining hands with others whose experiences and skills have prepared them to deal with problems which are beyond his competence. But knowledge of these resources is only part of the picture. In addition, there must be an understanding of what is involved in a valid use of this knowledge. This would include an approach to the professions or agencies involved and the enabling of the parishioner to avail himself of the services provided.

It is to a consideration of these issues that attention is given in the following pages. Chapter One introduces the problem, giving particular attention to the varieties of situations which may overtax the personal resources of the pastor, and examining briefly the kinds of help available to the pastor in dealing with these situations. Chapter Two begins by discussing some of the personal factors in referral, then turns specifically to the question, "When to Refer?" Chapters Three and Four respectively deal with the questions "How to Refer?" and "Where to Refer?" Included in the latter is a description of the major resources available to the pastor in assisting his parishioners to find the help they need. Chapter Five takes up some special problems including the matter of privileged communication and what happens when the referral does not work out. Chapter Six concludes the discussion by considering the on-going ministry of the pastor with the parishioner, after the particular difficulty which was the occasion for the referral has passed.

Preface to the Second Edition

The decision to republish a volume that has gone out of print is based upon the conviction that the material continues to be useful and, thus, should be available to the persons who can profit by it. I believe that this is the case with this book which first appeared over a decade ago in hard binding, and later was reprinted in a paperback edition. Words come to me from friends and colleagues that suggest there is still a need for seminary students and ministers to have access to the principles and processes described here.

As far as I know, this is the only book on referral as such that has appeared in my lifetime. To be sure, many books on pastoral care include sections or chapters on referral; but none, to my knowledge, deals solely with this crucial aspect of the minister's care of parishoners. Thus, when I was approached by Abingdon to consider the possibity of re-issuance, I was pleased to do so, and trust that my impression regarding the continuing usefulness proves to be correct.

My first thought, naturally, was to revise the entire text. After consultation with the publishers, however, it became evident that the cost of resetting the book would greatly increase the retail price and thus, in some sense, make the material less accessible. It is clear that the basic principles of referral have not changed in the twelve years since I wrote the manuscript during the winter of 1965–66. As C. S. Lewis notes in the preface to *The Screwtape Letters*, troubles seem to work without a timetable. The world scene shifts and changes, but personal struggle and distress have about them a timelessness that transcends the cultural situation of the moment. Thus, in the interest of economy and availability, I was willing to let the material stand.

Two factors, however, require comment in regard to this decision. In the first place, the material in chapter 4, "Where to Refer" has been brought up to date in regard to addresses, phone numbers, and other relevant data. As I checked with the various agencies and resources listed in the first edition, I was surprised to discover how few of the notations still remain unchanged. This suggests that even with the up-date of the present edition, the minister will need to verify addresses and phone numbers from time to time.

The second factor has to do with masculine/feminine language. It amazes me as I read the text to contemplate how far we have come in the past twelve years. In the mid-sixties our issues were the war in Viet Nam, civil rights, and the like. It is gratifying that the war is now history, and that we have moved forward in regard to civil rights, even though much is still to be done. In these intervening years our consciousness of the place of women in all aspects of life has been heightened, a perspective we have long needed. As I write this, supporters of the Equal Rights Amendment are pressing the Virginia General Assembly for ratification. And in the 1970s, women comprise some one-fourth to one-third of seminary students. While there is still no widespread readiness on the part of many churches to receive women ministers, we have made genuine progress.

Thus, as I read in this book such phrases as ". . . the minister . . . he . . ." it is difficult to believe that so short a time ago as 1966 this kind of terminology passed unnoticed. Such is no longer the case, and for that we can take heart. I still wrestle with the "he/she" type of unwieldiness with which our language burdens us. I believe we should be able to devise a solution such as "se" for "he/she," "hir" for "him/her," and "hes" for "his/her." My pessimistic hunch is that it will take us awhile to work out of the dilemma.

It is certain that the language difficulty is significant in and of itself. But this is the case precisely because it calls attention to the necessity for a change in attitude, a new awareness of the way we have moved beyond our distorted perceptions of the past. The fact is that the linguistic transition does in a basic fashion represent such a change, and that is all to the good. Thus, we go forward doing the best we can with the structures of language that we now have, and search not only for new terminology but also for new perspectives.

So it is that the decision not to re-set the entire book means that the language in use a decade ago remains. I trust that my colleagues in ministry, both women and men, will be able to read the text for its content rather than be turned aside by its masculine pronouns and patterns. And I also trust that these colleagues will join me in rejoicing that we have come so far in such a relatively short period of time.

Contents

CHAPTER—1
You Are Not Alone

There is a loneliness in the ministry. It is the kind of loneliness which is shared by everyone in professional life who daily finds himself confronted with issues and problems for which there is no "blueprint." It is a loneliness which wells up whenever decisions must be made that affect the lives of others, and for which there can be no definite assurance as to the final outcome. It is a loneliness which becomes increasingly poignant for the minister who realizes that he deals with time and eternity—that the questions put to him have to do with life and death and life again. It is a loneliness which tends to overwhelm when it emerges in a realistic consciousness of personal inadequacy.

There are some ministers who find the burden of this loneliness too great to bear. As a consequence, they may attempt to deny its reality by turning to some kind of authoritarian procedure which they hope will answer all the questions before they are asked, will provide a formula or strategy for dealing with every eventuality before it arises, and will assure success whatever the difficulty. Others may endeavor to escape the loneliness by concluding that nothing can be done; that there are no answers; that the questions may be considered in a kind of eternal vacuum, but that no conclusions are to be expected. The former tend to attempt everything with no regard for the realistic limitations imposed by life itself; the latter tend to attempt nothing with no regard for the realistic opportunities afforded by life itself. In the end, both such attempts are doomed to failure.

Quite in distinction to these reactions is the minister who knows the loneliness as a realistic fact, yet has come to experience in the presence of this genuine loneliness a genuine relationship which makes the loneliness not only bearable but also creative. At its deepest level, this relationship is both vertical and horizontal. The vertical dimension is the sure promise of the One who said, "Lo, I am with you always, to the close of the age." (Matthew 28:20, R.S.V.) The horizontal dimension is the daily awareness of the strength which comes in the company of those who "bear one another's burdens, and so fulfill the law of Christ." (Galatians 6:2, R.S.V.)

Varieties of Problems

It would, of course, be quite incorrect to imply that the three categories of ministers are separate and distinct; the fact is that there is some of each in every minister, more of one at times than others. In the situations which follow, it is probable that each minister who reads these words can sense within himself the extent to which one or another of these responses tends to be dominant; if so, such an awareness may lead to his individual next step in the pursuit of becoming increasingly helpful to parishioners in distress.

A disturbed student.[1]   The very ring of the telephone had a strident note of urgency.

"It's for you, George." She walked back into the dining room. "I wish people wouldn't call you while we're eating. But whoever this is, he really sounds upset."

"This is George Bowden." Through the years he had learned that troubles do not come on a timetable, that it is impossible to schedule human distress and misery.

"Can you come now? I've got to talk to you!"

"I'll be glad to come and help if I can. Can you tell me where you are?"

"I'm in the library. Hurry!"

"Don't hang up. Tell me a little more so I'll know how to find you.

---

[1] The case material used in this book is drawn from actual experiences. However, in each instance all identifying data have been changed or removed to insure the complete protection of the persons involved.

I want to come, but I don't want to lose any time looking in the wrong place."

"I'll be at the table by the door of the reading room. I'm supposed to be in class at two, but I can't go now. I don't think I can stand it much longer. They just ought not to do it. It's not right! It's not right! Hurry!"

He heard the click of the receiver. It would take twenty minutes to reach the college. Time enough to worry about the student after he got there; concentrate on the traffic, now. No use. His mind raced ahead. What would he find? He'd seen the boy in church on several occasions and at the College Group on Sunday evenings. Yet obviously he didn't really know him. Why had he called? Something, somewhere had indicated that help was available. Or had it? How could he be sure?

He walked into the library and started toward the reading room. He could feel the tension as he opened the door.

"They've no right to do it!" There was a kind of frantic urgency in the student's voice as he stood to meet him. "I won't stand for it any longer!"

"Let's go outside where we can talk," he said, gently. They walked together into the foyer.

"I'm the only one in the entire Freshman class who is studying the assignments in history. I work and work, and just as I get the facts clearly in mind, someone passes by my desk and draws them out. It's just like they had a magnet! All they need to do is walk by me, and they just pick them right out of my brain! It was bad enough when only one or two did it, but now they're all doing it! And I don't intend to keep it up; I can't carry the load for the whole class! The next one that does it, I'll get!"

There was an intensity in his voice which matched the force of the words.

"I just wanted you to know why I'm doing it."

Faced with such a situation, the most naive of pastors would realize that far more was needed than a summary dismissal of the student's complaint on the grounds that it was physically impossible and thus quite foolish. Indeed, the very conviction with which the words were said would be indication enough that their logical absurdity bespoke real distress within the person himself. If the more

sophisticated pastor suspected the presence of some paranoid delusions, his task would be no more simple because of this perception.
The crucial issue in either case would be the response of the pastor to
a cry for help which was not couched in terms of a plea. Nowhere
could the "Now I *have* got a problem; what am I going to do with
you? or for you? or to you?" be more clearly illustrated than in this
brief vignette.

In the moment of crisis all manner of possible actions present
themselves in rapid succession and just as rapidly seem to be dismissed as inadequate. What to do? Where to turn? As George
Bowden reflected on the situation in retrospect, he remembered
wondering why the student had called him. Why not his professor?
Why not the Dean of the college? Later, he remembered wondering
why the student had called anybody. Why had he not simply put
into effect his announced intention to "get" the next person who
"does it"?

It is in the moment of crisis that the loneliness is most acute. Is
there someone to call? Someone to assume part of the burden of the
difficulty. In the case of George Bowden, the answer was much more
simple than it is for the ordinary pastor. Being in a college community and dealing with a college student, he had access to the
academic as well as the administrative personnel of the community.
Yet this was not the entire answer, since the very fact that the
student had not called anyone connected with the college indicated
that somewhere within him there was a resistance to their being of
help. More was needed than a superficial suggestion that the student
get in touch with the Dean who could then take proper steps to
straighten the matter out. Moreover, Pastor Bowden recognized that
the student would probably need professional help, at least to the
extent of determining whether or not the situation was as serious as it
appeared to be. Thus, while he realized that it was not his place to
diagnose in the strict sense of the term, he was nevertheless aware of
the fact that he was already forming an evaluative judgment in his
own mind on the basis of which his relationship to the student would
be projected.

Inevitably his own feelings were very much a part of his approach to the situation. There was, of course, the genuine desire to be of help, to do the kind of thing which would be of value in some way or other toward enabling the student to resolve his difficulty. Alongside of this, however, there were other kinds of feelings. "What will happen if I do the wrong thing? I know that paranoid people are supposed to be dangerous. Is it possible that this student will attack me? What right do I have to call a psychiatrist? Is this not the responsibility of the college? Or the student's family? What reason do I have for believing a psychiatrist should be called at all? Maybe someone else should make this decision."

In the tangle of questions and uncertainties there is the clear conviction that some kind of additional help is going to be needed. Thus, the matter here is not whether to refer, but where and how. Indeed, the very presence of strong inner feelings of uncertainty and inadequacy is a sure indication that referral is necessary.

When a child is not normal.   "There's something wrong with the baby."

George Graves could fairly feel the pathos and the anguish in the words. Through the months of expectation he had called often on the Wilsons and had seen their eagerness in the realization that at last they were to have a child.

"I'm not sure I understand."

"I don't either. But he's not responding normally. There's nothing wrong with him physically, at least not as far as they can tell. It's . . . it's . . ."

He searched for words, but none came.

"The doctor isn't sure, yet. It may be brain damage, but he doesn't know to what extent. What are we going to do?"

It was the kind of question which permitted no answer. He knew that. He also knew that he wanted to have an answer more than anything else in the world. An answer that would be more than a cliché, more than superficial words of reassurance that had no roots in reality.

"What does the doctor say?"

Even as he asked the question, he realized that it had no meaning. Whatever the reply, the grinding misery was still the same. Yet he had to ask, mainly because he could think of nothing else to do.

"Only that we'll have to wait and see. He spoke of a clinic at the state capitol where specialists can do certain tests and tell more accurately about the situation. But we need to know now."

In a strict manner of speaking, the matter of referral is not the primary pastoral problem in this situation. Rather, the pastor is faced with the responsibility of enabling his parishioners to deal with the disappointment and heartache which come with the realization of mental retardation in one's own child. Nevertheless, once this has been done, there are certain constructive steps which can be taken—steps which include not only the resources of a consultation and evaluation clinic, but also the advantages and opportunities afforded by associations for retarded children.

In this process the pastor is not necessarily the primary source of information, athough he may actually have access to data not possessed by the parents of the child. In all likelihood, the pastor and the family physician will work together to assist in the parent's taking advantage of the services presently available. If such is the case, the role of the minister may well be that of enabling the parents to work through their feelings about the birth of a retarded child and thus assist in their decision to take whatever steps seem indicated to assure the best possible course of action for all concerned.

In this instance the pastor's knowledge of the progress that has been made in help for the mentally retarded and their parents would be of inestimable value at the point of reassurance and realistic assessment of opportunities.

An alcoholic. The time was 4:45 in the morning. The minister looked around the kitchen to see if there were any cups remaining that had not long since been used and allowed to dry out with the dregs of stale coffee crusted at the bottom. Apparently there wasn't a clean dish anywhere.

He had been aroused from sleep to hear the voice on the telephone asking if he would come immediately. He recognized the voice instantly. After dressing hurriedly, he drove the seven or eight miles to the country estate of the caller. As he drove, he could picture in his mind's eye what he would find. Yet when he was admitted, after prolonged ringing of the doorbell, the condition was worse than he had imagined. Norman had been drunk or drinking for nearly three weeks. Long since, his wife had taken the two children and gone to stay with her family. The house was a shambles.

"Come on in, Reverend."

They picked their way through the litter of newspapers, overflowing ashtrays, beer cans, and overturned chairs until they came to the kitchen.

"Come on, Reverend; let's get a cup o' coffee."

Norman was a big man. At that moment he was sober enough to know what he was saying, and drunk enough not to care. They scraped out two cups, filled them with black coffee, and sat down at the kitchen table.

"I suppose you think I didn't know what you were doing in my office."

The minister's thoughts went back to the day, now several months ago. He had gone to Norman's office on the insistence of his brother, who hoped something might be done about his alcoholism. It had been a ticklish situation at best. Norman was not a member of the minister's congregation, but they were more than slight acquaintances. In the days that followed, the minister reflected on what had happened. He'd not said anything about alcohol or drinking; indeed the talk had been quite superficial from one point of view. They'd talked of fishing, of new model cars that had just come on the market, and of mutual friends. Looking back, he'd wondered whether he should have been more straightforward, and came to feel that if he had it to do over again, he'd simply say why he was really there. As it was, he'd left with no more than a casual word that if Norman ever needed him, all he had to do was call. Well, he'd called.

"You thought you'd fooled me, talking about fishing and cars and no telling what else! I knew why you were there; and I wanted to pick up a chair and break it over your head! I still don't know why I didn't, and I may do it right now!"

For a moment, it seemed to the minister that Norman was about to make good his threat.

"You really resented my coming, and it makes you mad right now as you think about it."

It was as though the floodgates had burst open. For the next few minutes, all the buried resentment, bitterness, hostility, frustration, and despair came pouring out. The words tumbled over each other, lurid, vitriolic, scathing. After a while, the storm subsided. Norman put his head down on the table.

"Reverend, as you can see, I'm in awful shape. Can you help me? Is there anything you can do for me?"

The problem of alcoholism is complex and baffling; and those who, for whatever reason, are called on to work with alcoholics, whether willingly or unwillingly, soon learn the frustrating lesson that compulsive drinking does not yield to fervent pleading or moralistic exhortation. On many occasions, as was the case in the situation just mentioned, the minister's help is sought by someone other than the alcoholic. A wife, a brother, a father, or perhaps an employer will ask that something be done before it is too late. The problem of initiating help for the alcoholic has been the subject of considerable debate. Alongside the conviction that until the alcoholic expresses a desire for help little if anything can be done is the growing recognition that the offer of help, if made in the right way, can encourage the alcoholic to seek it.

In retrospect, the minister in this illustration felt that his initial visit to Norman could have been greatly improved. The fact was, however, that his going was in and of itself the indication of genuine concern and a willingness to help, coupled with a willingness to allow Norman to respond on his own terms. When, at last, he called, the time was right for something constructive to happen.

The call itself was both an end and a beginning. It was the end of Norman's attempting to delude himself into believing that he was able to control his drinking on his own initiative; it was the beginning of an openness to receive help in reconstructing his life along more positive lines. For the minister also, the call was an end and a beginning. It was the end of proffering help on a timetable suitable to Norman; it was the beginning of putting into practice the help that had been promised. Thus, the final statement and question posed by Norman was both an opportunity and a challenge. Granted that it is possible to help the alcoholic only when he recognizes his need of help, what is to be done when this point arrives? It is here that the minister finds allies in such groups as Alcoholics Anonymous, which have demonstrated the ability to enable the alcoholic to attain sobriety. There is tremendous value in the minister's having already become well acquainted with members of AA prior to the situation described in the illustration.

The Minister's Dilemma

The recounting of situations where the minister's knowledge of resources for referral is of prime importance for the welfare of his parishioners could go on indefinitely. The three illustrations given here, however, indicate the kinds of circumstances in which the need for such an understanding exists. In the first case, the call came directly from the person in distress, a person whose behavior definitely indicated the necessity for professional help. In the second case, the persons involved were already receiving professional help but discovered that something more than what might be called routine medical procedures were now required. In the third illustration, the initial call for help came from a third person. No account is given of the minister's relationship to the brother of the alcoholic, although it is entirely possible that he may have been one of the crucial factors in bringing help to the one obviously in distress. Even so, when the time finally came for direct help to the alcoholic, the minister knew that something more was needed than that which he could do by himself.

Thus far, there has been no indication of what the minister actually did in any of the situations recounted. The purpose here has been to set forth the circumstance in which ordinarily there would be the realization that additional help was needed. It is clear, however, that no hard and fast line can be drawn regarding the place of demarcation between the situation in which any particular minister feels capable of providing whatever help is required and one in which he feels the need to call upon someone else. What, for example, would have been the response if the student had described his condition as not being able to keep up with his studies, that he found himself procrastinating, falling farther and farther behind? I can recall such a situation in which the minister felt perfectly capable of helping the student to organize his life more effectively and to make better use of his time. It is probable that most ministers who read this would tend to believe that such a problem was one in which they could be of constructive help on their own. Yet, in the instance of this one student, the very organization of his life seemed to be the goad which precipitated a drastic crisis. Within a short time he was arrested on a morals charge and was expelled from the college. In retrospect, it seemed possible that his behavior regarding his studies was indicative of the inner turmoil that he was experiencing, a turmoil that began to emerge as he engaged in psychiatric treatment. He felt that he should withdraw from school, yet found it impossible to do because of family pressures. Presumably the poor grades might be the means of his being dismissed on academic grounds. As it turned out, the minister applied his attention to the raising of the grades; and as a consequence the student had "no alternative" but to engage in a behavior so obviously negative that the expulsion from the college would occur.

It would be purely speculative to suggest that had the minister enlisted the help of someone skilled in psychiatric therapy the crisis for this student might have been averted. Surely, no one would suggest that every student having difficulty with academic work should undergo psychotherapy. The point is that in many instances the presenting symptom is not so drastic as immediately to remind the minister of his inability to deal with the situation. We shall discuss the question of when to refer in a later chapter. It is sufficient for now to indicate that not every situation requiring referral is immediately visible in the first encounter between the minister and the parishioner.

Emerging Resources for Human Ills

We began this chapter by recognizing that there is a loneliness in the ministry, the kind of loneliness which comes in any professional experience where there are no hard and fast guidelines. We noted that the fact of this loneliness tended to drive some ministers toward a devaluation of their own abilities so that they were fearful of attempting help which they might responsibly give. At the same time, we suggested that this loneliness tended to drive some ministers to an overvaluation of their own resources, so that they were reluctant to call for help when it was desperately needed. Perhaps it has been possible for the ministers reading these words to sense the tendency which is most characteristic of their own reaction to the cry for help. In a later chapter, we shall explore these personal and inner responses at greater length.

One of the most promising factors emerging in the post-World War II era is the growing recognition of the values in a "team" approach to the ills of man. In the earlier decades of this century various disciplines and groups often manifested an exclusive imperialism—a feeling that they, alone, had the key to the distresses of man, and that all else was somehow secondary if not irrelevant in dealing with human suffering. More recently the helping professions have begun to come of age, to recognize that there are many facets to the human situation, that in joining hands there is the possibility of a more constructive and responsible approach.

The path toward such a cooperative effort has not been smooth. I can remember a consultation some fifteen years ago, in which I was a participant, which called together for three days a dozen persons representing as many groups or professions which were attempting to be of help to people in distress. There was a medical doctor, a psychiatrist, a psychologist, a sociologist, a psychiatric social worker, a nurse, a psychiatric aide, a lawyer, a teacher, a minister, a dentist, and a hospital chaplain. The only agenda was a frank and free discussion in which each participant in turn set forth the distinctive thing that he saw himself and his profession providing toward the alleviation of suffering, and the way he saw the members of the other professions related to what he was doing—if at all. As would be imagined, the comments and discussions were varied and provocative. Time and time again one person's description and definition of another was challenged. Certain self-defined areas for help were hotly contested by other participants who felt that their discipline had a kind of proprietory right to this or that aspect of human behavior. Some of the participants saw themselves dealing with only a limited and rather sharply prescribed aspect of mankind's ills. Others saw themselves in some way responsible for all of life despite the fact that in certain instances they were willing to concede that something other than their ministrations might be needed temporarily. There were occasions when the representative of one group called into question the very basis or right to existence of another group on the ground that what was done by the group could be better accomplished by others. And so the discussion continued for three days.

Although there was no intended conclusion to be reached as a result of the consultation and certainly no set of resolutions or findings that would be binding on anyone or any group, certain factors tended to stand out quite clearly as the discussions proceeded. The first, and perhaps most obvious, was that no one person could adequately represent or speak for any profession or group. Although the members of the consultation had been selected with some care to insure that their comments would be based on more than purely subjective impression, it was readily apparent that the position taken by any participant at any given time might or might not reflect a general consensus of the profession to which he belonged. Thus, it became increasingly evident that to make the statement "Psychology says thus and so," or "Theology holds this or that," is literally impossible. There are psychologists who say thus and so, and theologians who hold this or that, but there is no general consensus which subsumes all members of any group other than the broad-range designation of a discipline.

Having said that, however, certain other factors emerged which were quite revealing. There was a tremendous difficulty in communication. Each participant had certain symbols and terms which were not readily understood by other participants; indeed, it was evident that in many instances the symbols and terms evoked a far different concept than intended by the speaker. Moreover, this difficulty in communication was not simply a matter of esoteric jargon, although that was present from time to time. Rather there was the different or peculiar use of the same terms and symbols which prevented a genuine exchange of ideas and concepts.

In addition to, or perhaps as a part of, the difficulty in communication was the defensiveness and suspicion which marked many aspects of the discussion. Time and time again certain points were argued with much more heat than light as one or another felt himself or his discipline under attack. On many occasions it was clear that the representative of one group had little understanding of what was being done by another, yet had serious question about members of that group undertaking anything other than very narrowly defined activities.

Since I was one of two representing theology or religion, my own observations inevitably reflect the personal bias of my own perspective. Nevertheless, it seemed to me that the ministry, broadly defined, was the most widely diffuse group represented and that the conception of the task and function of the ministry held by the other representatives was the least clearly defined aspect of the conference. There were those who were frankly and overtly hostile toward the ministry in general. They felt that in most instances the minister probably did more harm than good when he attempted to be of help to people; indeed, one representative expressed the conviction that the clergy through the years had "stayed in business" by the constant creation of guilt feelings in their parishioners followed by offering a relief in the form of salvation from that which would not even have existed were it not for the Church! Their conclusion was that the greatest contribution which could be made to the welfare of mankind would be for the Church and the clergy to disappear completely! On a somewhat less radical scale, many members of the consultation expressed bewilderment at the great discrepancy which seemed to exist among various clergymen in regard to preparation and training. Since their own disciplines of medicine, psychology, psychotherapy, etc. had fairly well-defined requisites, they were puzzled by the fact that one clergyman might be a graduate of a university while another might have little, if any, formal education.

At the end of the consultation, there was general consensus that some such device or devices should be found to enable the varied helping groups to meet together from time to time in order that the resources of each might be understood and taken into account in dealing with the ills of mankind. Indeed, it was apparent even in the brief span of three days how the suspicion and hostility between certain representatives began to dissolve in growing understanding and recognition of mutual involvement in human suffering. In more recent years such conversations have been carried out on a much broader scale by such groups as the Academy of Religion and Health, the Commissions on Faith and Health established by several religious denominations, the Committee on Religion and Health set up by the American Medical Association, and many others.

Out of these discussions and forums has come the assurance to the pastor that he is not alone, that there are powerful allies who join with him in combating the distresses and ills which beset the members of his congregation and parish. It is because the manner and means for understanding and making use of these allied resources is not always readily apparent that this book is written. Perhaps as a consequence, more pastors will be able to draw on the resources which are at hand to the end that his people can find the way to a more abundant life.

CHAPTER—2
When To Refer

In the first chapter we learned that the minister has a host of professional persons who are able to participate in his working with those of his congregation who suffer distress. At the same time we were made aware that there are personal factors which raise various problems for the ministers who might make use of these resources.

Referral: Too Soon or Too Late

On the one hand, there are those ministers who are too quick to refer, failing to realize the potentiality of their own relationship to the parishioner. In the first chapter we noted that this kind of procedure often came about as a consequence of the pressure of loneliness in making decisions with regard to others. At this point it is possible to look a bit deeper into this sort of response to discover some of the aspects which make it characteristic of certain ministers.

First of all, many ministers have often heard the warning that the primary responsibility in pastoral care and counseling is to recognize the situations in which their principal duty is referral. Since the emergence of pastoral counseling as one of the major activities of the minister there has been a concern lest the pastor think of himself as a sort of "psychiatrist, J. G." Literature and lecture halls have been full of illustrations of the minister who mistakenly believed that he was able to help the parishioner suffering from severe headaches only to discover at her death that she had died of a brain tumor! In like manner, every minister has been cautioned against attempting diagnostic procedures for which his training and experience left him ill fitted.

As a consequence of these warnings, not a few ministers have felt a genuine fear of being found at fault when something went wrong in the life of the parishioner whom they were attempting to help. What, they wondered, would people think if this person actually committed suicide? What would the community think if these persons separated and got a divorce? What would be the impression if it were known that this parishioner engaged in homosexual practices?

Let it be said that the concern is a genuine one. As one minister put it, "It would be just as foolish for me to attempt to help a homosexual as it would be for me to attempt to remove a diseased appendix!" At the same time, there can be no facile neglect of the power of the Gospel to effect a change in the life of every man. This does not mean that there can be a cavalier disregard for the skills and experiences of those whose training has fitted them to deal with particular distresses of man. It does mean that the minister needs to be prepared to take seriously the fact that faith can indeed move mountains.

As I write these words, I find myself wishing that it were possible to speak personally with each one who will read them. In my imagination I can picture those who take comfort in the affirmation of the power of the Gospel and who are, as a consequence, encouraged to neglect their responsibilities to participate in and cooperate with those who engage in the healing arts. It is through this kind of distortion that all manner of excesses have emerged in what has been falsely termed "faith healing," when this concept has been defined as any healing that seems to be set over against the regular procedures of medical science. The plain fact is that all healing is at root a mystery, whatever the overt or tangible agent. It is in this sense that I would resist any indication of encouraging those who seek some confirmation in their disregard of the sciences of medicine and psychotherapy.

At the same time, I can also imagine those who begin to question the propriety of the minister dealing with persons whose distress is serious by any responsible criterion. Is it not, they would ask, too risky for the minister to attempt to heal the potential suicide? Should the minister not recognize the incipient psychotic and forthwith make arrangements for the person to be seen by a psychiatrist? The only honest answer, of course, is that there is genuine risk in any intervention in the life of another person but that the ministry of the Gospel is not in any sense designed to protect the minister from any and all risks. If it is true that the ills of man stem ultimately from his separation from himself, his fellows, and his God, then it is also true that these ills will never be overcome apart from the reestablishment of those relationships which have been broken or distorted. It is in this sense that the minister will certainly be desirous of taking advantage of every advance of the healing arts discovered through years of painstaking research and practice; but at the same time, he will recognize that his ministry to those who suffer the pains of the body and of the spirit is no less significant than that of those who make available the remedies of empirical research.

Thus far we have been arguing that some ministers are too quick to refer by reason of their inability or unwillingness to take seriously the implications of the Gospel for the relief of the suffering of mankind. On the opposite side of the coin there is the fact that other ministers are much too slow in referring those whose situation requires the specialized assistance of one trained in the healing arts. This hesitation to refer may stem from any number of causes.

For some, there is the feeling that the Gospel should be adequate to meet the needs of all sorts and conditions of men. For them, any referral is in and of itself an admission that the Gospel is inadequate. In its more extreme form this sort of attitude manifests itself as a refusal to accept medical aid in any form whatsoever. Quite apart from that, however, is the feeling that somehow the ministry of the Church should be sufficient to deal with neurotic or psychotic conditions, should be adequate to resolve all the problems of personal relationships, should be able to provide an answer to every situation. Alongside this notion is the personal feeling on the part of some ministers that they should be able to deal with every situation presented to them. There is the fear that any attempt to refer a parishioner to another professional person is a tacit admission of their own inability or weakness.

In this sort of feeling there is, of course, a constricted notion of the Gospel which confines it to those forms and symbols which can be identified as theological on their face. In addition, there is the personal threat that someone else may be as capable, if not more so, in meeting the problems of life than oneself. There is here a reminder of the attitude recorded in the Gospel according to Luke. "John answered, 'Master, we saw a man casting out demons in your name, and we forbade him, because he does not follow with us.' But Jesus said to him, 'Do not forbid him; for he that is not against you is for you.'" (Luke 9:49, 50) The obvious point is that the Gospel works through many forms which may not immediately be recognized but which are valid nonetheless.

From time to time I hear theological students and ministers take the position that the referral of a person to a psychiatrist is a betrayal of the Gospel. The argument runs that the person should be able, through faith and prayer, to gain the strength to meet any situation with which he is confronted. The fallacy in such a position is the unwillingness or the inability to recognize that God works through many channels, not all of which are readily identifiable as "religious." In like manner there is the unwillingness or the inability to take seriously man's necessity to utilize all manner and forms of healing which have been developed, as a consequence of searching out the laws of health which are inherent in the order of creation.

In the discussion of those who were too quick to refer, I indicated a desire to be able to meet personally those who read these words and, thus, to engage in meaningful dialogue with them. I find the same feeling here. It is possible that the reader begins to feel that the view of the Gospel set forth in this section loses the kind of uniqueness which is part and parcel of the faith of the Church. It should be said that there is validity in this concern. Nevertheless, there is the constant necessity for a recognition that God is at work in the most unlikely of places and that recognition of His presence is not the final criterion for determining the essential validity of the process or the extent of His participation.

Quite apart from these feelings of threat to the self or to the Gospel, there are those who are slow to refer precisely because they have no ready access to the resources for referral or because they are unaware of the possibilities for healing available to them in the various healing professions. It is certainly true that many communities do not possess the wide variety of specialized services which are the common lot of metropolitan areas. Even so, in this day of rapid transportation there are few persons who need to be deprived of professional help by reason of distance or inaccessibility.

A much more telling obstacle to referral is the mistrust of the minister regarding the world-view or orientation of the professional person. This is not so much the case with regard to the medical doctor as it is with regard to the psychiatrist. How often is it true that the minister feels that his parishioner will have "all his religion psychoanalyzed out of him"? Was not Freud, he asks himself, an atheist? Are not many psychiatrists irreligious if not antireligious? It is interesting that these same sorts of questions are not ordinarily raised regarding one who is to remove a diseased appendix or to deliver a baby. They seem to become a factor when the parishioner is wrestling with some personal problem such as compulsive behavior or deep depression.

It is probable that this kind of feeling is closely linked with the minister's feeling of threat that he is inadequate or that the Gospel is inadequate to deal with all sorts and conditions of men. In essence, the same kinds of principles are applicable here, also. The power of God is not limited to those channels which overtly attest to His presence; nor is healing any less a matter of faith, even though certain theological symbols are not in evidence.

Finally, there are certain ministers who are slow to refer simply because they do not understand the process involved in bringing the parishioner into touch with some other professional person who is better able to meet his needs. Having experienced the parishioner's feeling of rejection when it was suggested that he see someone else, the pastor is hesitant to raise the issue lest it seem that he is no longer desirous to be of help.

In this brief scope I have attempted to deal with some of the major feelings which make the minister either too quick or too slow to refer his parishioners to some other source of help. In every instance the focus has been upon the feelings of the minister himself. Because of this fact, it is likely that many who read this discussion will find it convenient to conclude that the responses described do not apply to them, although they may be able to identify the feelings as true of fellow ministers. If this is the case, then the discussion will be fruitless. Unless each minister is able to perceive the kinds of tendencies which ordinarily mark his own response to the plea for help, it is not likely that there will be any significant improvement in his relationship to his parishioners or to those whose profession equips them to deal with specific conditions. On the other hand, if there is a realistic recognition of this or that aspect of referral or its distortion as pertaining to the ordinary feeling of each particular reader, then there is a genuine possibility for growth.

Basic Principles

One of the thorniest problems in the work of the minister is the determination of when the situation of a parishioner who has sought his help is beyond his range of ability and therefore requires referral. Everyone agrees that such conditions exist; few agree as to their exact definition.

Recently, I participated in a seminar made up of physicians and clergymen whose purpose it was to explore the relationship which existed between their two professions and to determine ways and means of closer cooperation. After a time of dealing in generalities and avowing that there was really no basic tension between the ministers and the doctors in that locality, the discussion began to center on the minister's role in dealing with people in trouble. One physician, engaged in the practice of internal medicine, expressed his position in no uncertain terms—the clergyman had no business attempting to be a psychiatrist and should certainly not become involved in anything that looked like psychotherapy. There was a general nodding of heads around the room as physicians and clergymen alike expressed their agreement with this broad thesis.

Nevertheless, as the discussion progressed, it soon became clear that there was no unanimity at all on what was actually meant by the phrases "attempting to be a psychiatrist," and "involved in . . . psychotherapy." One clergyman, who expressed his own agreement with the statements, asked the physican if he would set forth a few guidelines on the basis of which the clergymen present might make the distinction when approached by a parishioner for help. Nearly a half hour went by, but no such guidelines were forthcoming. There were many generalities. "The minister should not attempt to diagnose mental illness or emotional distress." "The minister should not attempt to deal with depth material." "The minister should not attempt a reconstruction of the personal dynamics of the individual." "The minister should not attempt to deal with deep depression." The list ran on and on.

After a time it became evident that there were general impressions but no particular points of reference. One by one the ministers present cited instances of pastoral interviews in which parishioners had manifested one or more strong negative feelings, such as a deep sense of guilt, bewilderment and grief, fierce anger or resentment, loneliness and isolation, jealousy, frustration, bitterness, and the like. In each instance there was the question, "Should this person have been referred to someone else for help?" And in each instance there was the reply, "It all depends." Then, in answer to the question, "Depends on what?" The replies trailed off into generalities again, "on the intensity of the feeling" or "on the disturbance of the person" or "on whether or not there is indication of mental illness."

It can be argued that in any other similar gathering there would certainly be those who could come up with more cogent and helpful answers than were produced in the seminar which I have been discussing. Nevertheless, I am convinced after many years of working with groups of clergymen in the area of pastoral care and counseling that the question of when to refer remains as ill defined as any other confronting the minister.

One possible reason for this lack of clarity stems from the fact that in most attempts to define the point of referral the emphasis is on the condition of the parishioner. Thus, it is stated, if the person is troubled only to such and such a degree, then the minister is justified in attempting to be of help; on the other hand, the argument runs, if the person is troubled to this or that intensive degree, then the minister should by all means refer. While there is a definite logic in such a formula, in that the condition of the parishioner must always be a basic factor in the decision to refer, the difficulty comes in that the situation of the minister is presumed constant throughout. When, however, the focus is on the minister rather than on the parishioner, it becomes possible to define certain principles which make the question of when to refer a bit more manageable. In the discussion which follows, three principles are presented, each of which has to do with a particular limitation on the part of the minister. In each instance, the thesis is that when the particular limitation is exceeded, the parishioner should be referred elsewhere for help. While it is granted that the situation of the parishioner is and must be a prime factor in the assessment, the focus is on the minister's assessment of himself in the presence of the parishioner and his problem. The three limitations are (1) time, (2) skill or experience, and (3) emotional reserve or stability.

1. *Limitation of time.* The proper apportionment of time is a continual problem for every parish minister. How much time shall he spend in sermon preparation, in parish visitation, in pastoral counseling, in congregational administration, in recreation, in study? Whatever the formula devised by any particular minister, it is inevitable that there never seems to be enough time to go around. By necessity, each aspect of his work must be curtailed to a certain extent simply because other essential responsibilities must be fulfilled.

Thus it is that on many occasions parishioners bring problems to the pastor which are within the scope of his skill and resources but for which he simply does not have sufficient time. This limitation of time may be situational or it may be structural. Illustrations of situational limitation include the obvious occasions when the pastor is to be out of town or when he finds his schedule filled with a series of appointments which cannot be set aside. In such instances his responsibility is to refer the parishioner to someone else who can make available sufficient time to deal with the problem.

The same principle, although not so obvious, applies also in regard to structural limitations. Here the parishioner requires large blocks of time over a considerable period. A gross illustration is hospitalization. Broadly defined, hospitalization is the provision of constant attention by skilled personnel under controlled conditions. Theoretically, if not actually, it might be possible for the pastor to provide many, if not most, of the constant care aspects of hospitalization by devoting himself twenty-four hours a day to this one parishioner. While such a notion is ridiculous on its face, it is indicative of the limitaton of time that is structural rather than situational. Since, obviously, the pastor cannot and should not devote all his attention to one parishioner and since it is not within his prerogative to effect hospitalization, his course is referral.

It can be argued that what is actually at stake here is the limitation of skill and experience, that the pastor lacks the personal resources as well as the time to deal with the distress of the parishioner. The fact is that these two often overlap and are separated here only for the sake of discussion. More particular attention is given to the limitation of skill and experience below. A more telling argument is that the real criterion here is the condition of the parishioner rather than the limitation of the pastor. Yet, once it is granted that these two are inevitably linked as two sides of the same coin, the principle which emerges in terms of the pastor's limitation provides a guideline for those situations which are not as obvious as hospitalization. The following verbatim reconstruction presented by a parish minister in a counseling seminar sets forth certain factors which illustrate the principle.

David and Joan

David and Joan are members of my parish with whom I have counseled from time to time. She has had a problem with drinking, and more recently has threatened to leave home and kill their three children so that when they were divorced he wouldn't get them. David asked me to come to the house as soon as possible. It was about 9:30 in the evening.

1. *Joan:* (answering my knock) Hello, Pastor. Come in.
2. *Pastor:* Thank you, Joan. Hello, David.

3. *David:* Hello. (silence)

4. *Pastor:* You asked me to come over, David. What seems to be wrong?

5. *Joan:* (breaking in immediately) He's asked me to get out, that's what! (silence) Isn't that right, David? Tell him you asked me to get out! Go ahead. Don't let the fact that he's a preacher stop you. (Then she shouted.) *Well, go ahead!*

6. *Pastor:* Did you ask her to leave, David?

7. *David:* Well (pause)—not exactly!

8. *Joan:* (loudly) You know damn well you did—now tell him what you said.

9. *David:* Well (short pause), all I said was that we couldn't go on this way.

10. *Joan:* Oh, hell, you said more than that—(again loudly) *now tell him what you said!*

11. *Pastor:* Please, Joan. Give him a chance.

12. *Joan:* O.K. (then quite meekly) I'll let you tell him, David.

13. *David:* All I said was that we couldn't go on like this, and that if Joan didn't straighten up that she might as well get the "H" (he didn't say "hell") out—that the kids and I would get along a lot better without her.

14. *Joan:* That's just what he told me! (then louder) and that's just what I'm going to do—soon as Bill (her brother) gets here! (Joan made several trips to the door and looked out, then she went to the kitchen and lit another cigarette. She had been smoking constantly from the time I entered the house—David likewise. She came back to the living room.)

15. *Pastor:* Joan, there must be some reason he asked you to leave. Do you know what it was? Do you want to talk about it?

16. *Joan:* There's nothing more to talk about. He told me to (loudly) *get the hell out,* and that's what I'm doing. Where's that Bill?

17. *David:* Now Joan, Reverend Jones came down here because I asked him to and because we need some help. Let's talk it over with him.

18. *Joan:* (loudly) *Oh, hell,* there's nothing to talk about. You want me out of the way, and I'm getting out. But when I leave, you

and your mother won't have the kids! (She was very determined at this point and threatening.)

19. *Pastor:* Are you coming back after the children, or are you planning to take them with you?

20. *Joan:* They're over at *his* mother's (with a sneer) now—I can't get them now; but they won't have them—not him or his mother. That's just what they want! (again she added, threateningly) But they won't get them, never!

21. *Pastor:* Why? (long silence, during which I watched them glare at one another several times)

22. *David:* Tell Reverend Jones what you told me.

23. *Joan:* (very threateningly and slowly) I'll kill them!

24. *Pastor:* You'll what?

25. *Joan:* (snapping back) You heard me! (then apologetically) I'm sorry. (She began to cry, but not for long.)

26. *Pastor:* Why did David ask you to leave? (a knock at the door, and Joan answered it)

27. *Joan:* Hello, Bill. Come in. I've been waiting. This is Reverend Jones from Bethel Church.

28. *Pastor:* Hello, Bill.

29. *Bill:* Hello. Hello, Joan. Hi, David. What's going on here?

30. *Joan:* David asked me to leave, and that's what I'm doing. Are you ready to go?

31. *Bill:* (realizing I was there to help) I'll have a cup of coffee first. O.K.?

32. *Joan:* Help yourself. (nervously) But for God's sake hurry it up. (Bill went to the kitchen and poured his coffee.)

33. *Pastor:* Won't you sit down, Joan, and let's talk about this a little?

34. *Joan:* Go ahead and talk—I can do better standing up.

35. *Pastor:* Just what brought all this on?

36. *David:* Joan got to drinking again. She just can't leave it alone. We'd be better off without her if she's going to be like this all the time.

37. *Joan:* Oh, yeah, it's all my fault. You don't have any faults at all!

38. *David:* Now, Joan. (tenderly) I didn't say that.

39. *Joan:* Why are you blaming me then?

40. *David:* I'm not saying it's all your fault.

41. *Joan:* Oh, hell, that's not what you said two hours ago.

42. *David:* But that was a long time ago.

43. *Joan:* Yes, but you said it! (shouting) *Bill, are you done with that coffee?*

44. *Bill:* (from the kitchen) Almost finished. Go ahead and talk. I think you ought to think this thing over. The reverend is here to help if you two will let him.

45. *Joan:* But it isn't all my fault. (silence)

46. *Pastor:* No one is saying it is, Joan.

47. *Joan:* But they might as well have.

48. *Pastor:* Now you don't really mean that, do you?

49. *Joan:* (as she sat on the arm of the divan—sitting for the first time) No, I don't. But he has faults, too.

50. *David:* I'll admit that.

51. *Joan:* Well, why don't you tell Reverend Jones some of yours then, instead of blaming me for everything?

52. *Pastor:* Do you want to name some of your faults, David? (long silence)

53. *Joan:* Go ahead, David. (almost demanding) Tell him your faults.

54. *David:* I know I'm not home enough. I know I don't give you enough of my time. I'm not the mushy, lovey type, as you think I ought to be. And I'm stubborn.

55. *Joan:* When *was* the last time you told me you loved me?

56. *David:* (after a bit of thought) I don't remember.

57. *Joan:* You're damned right you don't—it's been that long ago! It was eight weeks ago yesterday! And the last time you kissed me was . . .

58. *David:* (breaking in) . . . day before yesterday!

59. *Joan:* Yeah, and that was just for a show because somebody else was here and you were leaving for the city.

60. *Pastor:* Is that right, David? (silence, and more silence—probably two full minutes) Why is it you're leaving, Joan?

61. *Joan:* 'Cause he told me to get out!

62. *David:* But I don't want you to, really!

63. *Joan:* But I'm going. Come on, Bill. (She got up again.)

64. *Bill:* In a minute.

65. *Pastor:* Joan, I don't think you really want to go. If I promise to come back in twenty hours, will you and David try to make out that long together?

66. *Joan:* He asked me to leave.

67. *Pastor:* David, I think you two can work this out for twenty hours. If I come back then will you try to get along for that length of time? I'm sure a good night's sleep will do all of us a lot of good.

68. *David:* I'm willing to try.

69. *Pastor:* How about you, Joan?

70. *Joan:* (very meekly and with a smile) I'll try.

71. *Pastor:* I'll be back then in twenty hours. See you then. Glad to have met you, Bill. 'Bye now.

In the seminar discussion of this pastoral report the minister involved made several significant observations. In the first place, he recognized that his intervention had been shaped by the crisis situation at hand and that he had not really dealt with the feelings of either David or Joan. He acknowledged that his primary purpose had been to "buy time," to postpone the actual break in the hope of being able to effect some kind of restorative or reconciling process. It was in this sense that he felt able to justify his frank manipulation in preventing Joan from leaving with Bill.

In line with this realization, the minister also noted that this interview, while more intense than any former one, tended to follow a definite pattern. On more than one occasion he had been asked to help resolve the marital tensions between David and Joan—and had been somewhat successful in smoothing over the ruffled places. The eruption of strong negative feelings in this interview, however, made it clear that much more was needed than a simple resolution of occasional spats.

During the twenty-hour interval, the minister had occasion to think back over his relationship to David and Joan and saw rather clearly the extent to which he had never really taken the time to deal with them as persons. As he described his feelings in the seminar he wasn't sure even then whether this circumstance was occasioned by his inability to deal with the negative feelings which were a part of their lives or a recognition that the time required to resolve the tangled feelings was more than he would manage. In any event, he was convinced that the factor of time was crucial, however much his uneasiness over Joan's threat to kill the children made him hesitant to continue alone. Thus, when he returned on the following evening, he had decided that his best course of action was to enable them to see a professional marriage counselor. In this instance, the minister reported that such a referral had been made, and that after several months the family situation seemed to be greatly improved. For our purpose here, the actual process whereby the referral was effected is not crucial. It is sufficient only to note that despite certain personal reservations regarding his ability to deal with the situation in which David and Joan found themselves, the primary reason for referral reported by the minister was a realistic lack of time to set up the prolonged interviews necessary to provide the needed assistance.

In my own parish ministry, I found the limitation of time indicating the necessity for referral most often in dealing with alcoholics. After several years of close association with Alcoholics Anonymous which included going with AA members on "12th Step Work," sitting up most of the night with someone suffering from withdrawal symptoms when literally no hospitalization was available, or working through the tangled resentments and bitter self-rejection which so often marked the path of the alcoholic who sought recovery, I came to feel that I was able to be of genuine help to those who suffered from this malady. Nevertheless, time and time again I felt it appropriate to refer the alcoholic to AA on two bases. In the first place, apart from some such referral it was actually possible that I would find myself doing nothing else but work with alcoholics. In the second place, the members of AA derived personal benefit from their own "12th Step Work" which was of tremendous value in their maintenance of sobriety.

Throughout these varied illustrations, the principle of limitation of time emerges as a point of reference for every minister. Referral is indicated when the pastor recognizes that his responsibilities prevent his spending the amount of time which seems necessary for the parishioner to work through his problem effectively and creatively. In the end, it is a decision which each minister must make for himself.

✝ *2. Limitation of skill or experience.* Throughout the discussion of the limitation of time it has been apparent that this factor is inextricably bound with the limitation of skill or experience. Yet, in every instance, there is a distinction. The primary consideration is the pastor's awareness that the parishioner is describing a situation or a feeling which seems not to be coherent or logical to him, or which transcends his personal experience.

The following illustrative contact was reported by a theological student who had returned to his home church to speak at a Wednesday evening service. Just prior to the beginning of the meeting, this student was standing in the foyer outside the auditorium when he was approached by a member of the congregation. He remembered having met him casually—and that he had experienced emotional difficulty in the past. No one else was present.

1. *Student:* Hello, Jack. It's good to see you. How are you?

2. *Jack:* (At this point Jack bent forward from the waist, putting his face lower than mine and peered up at me as though he was not sure who I was.) Oh, it's o.k. now. You don't look like you used to look. Funny we should meet right here.

3. *Student:* Why is that, Jack?

4. *Jack:* This is where we first met years ago.

5. *Student:* Why, that's right, Jack. I'm glad you remembered. How are you getting along?

6. *Jack:* Oh, all right. Say, this is kinda sudden, but do you know that I think I can stop that war?

7. *Student:* What do you mean, Jack?

8. *Jack:* That war where people are getting killed, where all that violence is going on. I can stop it. I feel God has "told" me to stop violence.

9. *Student:* You mean the war over in Vietnam?

10. *Jack:* Yes, yes! I've had things happen to me. I've stopped fights right here in our town. The other day I found two fellas

fighting in a drug store, and I walked up to them and without putting a hand on them I said, "You fellas are sure acting immature." And they stopped fighting right away.

11. *Student:* Ummmm.

12. *Jack:* Everybody, including you, is *doing something.* I'm not doing anything.

13. *Student:* You feel, then, that God has called you to stop people from harming themselves and others, and that you will achieve a real goal in your life by doing this.

14. *Jack: Yes,* I feel like just hoping that some kind of violence will happen so I can stop it. (At this point his hands were out in front of him, and he was almost acting out the role he was telling me about.)

15. *Student:* Jack, when you see Reverend Williams, talk this over with him. Perhaps he may be able to offer some suggestions which would be of help to you.

16. *Jack:* Oh, I already have. (At this point it was time to go into the Chapel and begin the service, thankfully!)

From the very beginning of this interview, the student felt uneasy. As a consequence, his attempt at referral in No. 15 was basically sound, although the procedure could be called into question. In discussing the matter later, he noted that he had been caught "flat-footed," despite the fact that he had known Jack for some years. He was obviously relieved when the actual pressure of schedule rescued him, since, as he put it, he had no idea what to do.

It can be argued that the several responses by the student left much to be desired, that at some point there was the necessity to indicate his own perception of the situation lest, inadvertently, he might tend to strengthen or confirm what he believes to be a distortion or delusion. From the standpoint of whether or not referral is indicated, however, this is irrelevant. It is true that a more appropriate procedure throughout might have increased the possibility for a successful referral, but here, again, the basic factors remain unchanged. What is at stake is that this person is describing his situation in terms which do not make sense to the student, terms which seem to him to represent an unrealistic perception of "things as they are."

When the matter is put this way, the crucial issue turns on the counselor's ability to recognize the limitations of his own skill and experience. Obviously, this factor will differ from person to person and, indeed, will change from time to time in the same person. The illustration in Chapter One of the student who felt that his fellow classmates were "drawing knowledge out of his head" would seem to describe a condition beyond the scope of the average pastor. Yet it is conceivable that the pastor might fail to make a proper evaluation and deceive himself into believing that he could deal with the problem on his own.

The matter becomes particularly complex when an attempt is made to define the term "proper evaluation." Consider the following case report which appeared in the *New Christian Advocate*[1] in February 1957.

A young man of about 21 with whom I was not acquainted called at my home.

1. *Youth:* I am a senior at _____ College. I am finding it very difficult to adjust to college life. I seem lost. I am trying to find out what to do and what to think. It all began last December. I began to feel as if I had lost something out of me. It seems as though I am losing consciousness of people about me. I can see them, but there is no depth of feeling. I spent two years at another college. In my first year there I had an indwelling of the Spirit. It came in softly. A voice said, "Feed my sheep." That was an answer to prayer. It settled my problem. God intended me to prepare for the ministry. I was hesitant about it. In the fall I got a draft blank. I stated I was a pre-theological student. Then in December, I don't know what happened. My sense of social consciousness went. I had an idea I shouldn't be in college. Final exams came up, and I got excited. Later I got depressed. I waited for an answer from God. I felt I should do something. I couldn't concentrate on my studies.

2. *Pastor:* Can you tell me some more about yourself?

[1] Copyright 1957 by Lovick Pierce, publisher.

3. *Youth*: Yes. Last week I had a terrific pain in my head. I thought I was losing control of my thoughts. I was blank at times. I talked with another pastor. He said I was tired out with too much study. He said I was experiencing transition from adolescence to adulthood. In the library I saw a book about a mother. It brought tears to my eyes. Then I was so conscious of myself that I withdrew from activities. Now I don't seem to have a sense of reality.

4. *Pastor*: It is hard for you to understand these things.

5. *Youth*: Yes. In my first year in college I heard a voice. It came from the outside. A voice came in. It put me at ease. It was wonderful—a coming in and being lifted up. It was in bed—I was nearly asleep. It seemed God wanted me to do something. Then later an empty feeling in my mind, a losing contact with reality. And I lost contact with God. I had no idea of companionship. Last week it was so bad I thought I should take some time off; so I came here. There seems to be such a distance between myself and other people.

6. *Pastor*: You are feeling rather cut off from others, is that it?

7. *Youth*: Yes. And sometimes it seems as though I am going to lose the power of speech. I have to think hard to find words to say. I find myself staring out into space. I fear I will be speechless and stare out to find words. Also, it seems at times that the world is going to come to an end. At the first college everyone seemed to have the idea that something big was coming. In religion there was so much emphasis on the social Gospel that there was no faith. The emphasis was on correcting social evils.

8. *Pastor*: And you did not agree with this emphasis.

9. *Youth*: No, there did not seem to be time. But lately time seems to be different. It seems to begin in the morning and end at night. There is no continuity. My calling to be a theological student seems faint. I seem to be losing my identity in this, and I am not finding any other identity. I had a silly notion that I was turning into an anti-Christ. It was silly—I gave it up—I wanted to vomit when I thought of it, and I have vomited a lot.

10. *Pastor*: These ideas seemed wrong to you.

11. *Youth*: Well, no, all ideas seem on the same level. There seems to be no difference in the meaning of words. But I get ideas

that I am not myself anymore; I am someone else. It is all so confusing.

As in the case of the student who met the parishioner just before the worship service, it is not our purpose here to examine the counseling procedure of this pastor. The point at issue is the matter of "proper evaluation" when seen from the perspective of the pastor. Rather than indicate what the conclusion of this pastor actually was, it might be more helpful for each pastor who reads this interview to ask himself what his own assessment is, and the basis upon which this assessment is made. Such questions as "Do I understand what he is saying?" "Do I understand what these things mean to him?" "Do I feel capable of responding to him in such a way that he can resolve these tensions which are disturbing him?" "Is my experience such that I can be confident that I will not misread or misinterpret his situation, or overlook some significant factor which could spell the difference between help and hindrance?" "Is my skill such that I can avoid the blunders which might prove disastrous for him?"

Of course, not every pastor will ask the questions in these ways, nor will every pastor answer these or similar questions in the same way. Moreover, it is inevitable that whatever answers are given will, of necessity, be highly subjective. The extent of the subjectivity emerges when and if the question "Do I feel comfortable with this person" becomes a major factor. It is, of course, true that if the pastor does not "feel comfortable" with the parishioner, there is little likelihood of his being much help to him. As can be seen clearly in the interview, between the student and the parishioner outside the Chapel, the fact that the student was ill at ease from the beginning made it inevitable that he would have to devote most of his energies to dealing with his own distress. Yet "feeling comfortable" is subject to the same treacheries as "proper evaluation."

It is not difficult to document the fact that many ministers have been taken off guard by a parishioner's use of theological terms to describe a personal experience which turned out to be quite pathological in nature. Many a minister might find himself somewhat hesitant to question a parishioner's description of some numinous or ecstatic experience of the presence of God, even though he found himself entertaining certain cautions as he listened. Somewhere along a continuum a point is reached beyond which the minister becomes convinced that the described experience is not creative but pathological.

In the first long statement by the college student who called on the pastor in the interview on page 45, there is a description of what appears to be a "religious experience." The fact that it is related in a context of apparent emotional disturbance may be sufficient for many pastors to conclude that here was a person needing more help than they could provide. For some, the fact that the student reports "A voice said, 'Feed my sheep'" would raise a flag of caution. It is possible that the same ministers might have reached a different conclusion if the statement had read, "In my first year I had an indwelling of the Spirit. It came softly, but there was a strong conviction that God intended me to prepare for the ministry. It was an answer to prayer, and it settled my problem." Disregarding the context, the only real difference is the omission of the words, "A voice said . . ."

Although it is apparent that there is no escape from the subjective factor in the minister's assessing his own limitations, this does not mean that the subjectivity is completely unrelieved by any objective point of reference. Certain generalizations provide possible guidelines for arriving at a conclusion which has more foundation than simple impression. Illustrations include behavior which is not typical of the person, behavior which does not seem to square with reality, behavior which is described as producing pain and distress from which there is no relief, behavior which seems to bring unrelieved pain or distress to the person's associates, and the like. It can be seen that in each of these instances more must be taken into consideration than the bare fact described. In addition, as we have already noted, different pastors are by reason of various experiences more or less prepared to respond helpfully to any given situation. In any event, the responsible pastor continuously checks his own subjective impressions precisely because his concern is to be of maximum help to his parishioners, rather than to maintain the illusion that his own impressions are always correct.

Thus far, we have discussed the indication for referral when the pastor recognizes a limitation of his own experience or skill. The illustrations have been of the sort which ordinarily apply to both concepts. It is possible, however, to separate the two in order to indicate the sense in which the minister might very well understand the situation by reason of previous experience, but might be unable to help by reason of lack of skill. A ridiculously obvious illustration might be the parishioner who requested the pastor to remove his diseased appendix! Such a parishioner, to carry the illustration out to a logical (or illogical) conclusion, might plead with the pastor stating that he trusted him, whereas he had a great distrust for all surgeons; that he was convinced that the pastor could be of much more help to him than any physician; and that if the pastor did not remove the appendix, he had no intention of seeking help elsewhere. In this farfetched account, it is conceivable that the pastor might very well understand what the physical condition being described entailed, while he questioned the judgment behind the parishioner's request. The plain fact, of course, is that he would not in any sense attempt such an operation even though he might have great sympathy for the parishioner's anguish. Never having been trained in surgery, he would know that however well intentioned his efforts, the results of his attempting the removal of an appendix could end only in disaster.

However ludicrous this illustration, the basic thesis becomes more disturbing when the condition being described by the parishioner is some sort of personal or emotional distortion, rather than a physical complaint. It is by no means as simple for many ministers to resist such a plea. Suppose, for example, the parishioner tells of being crushed by deep depression and despair or being troubled by visions and voices which prevent sleep and fill his life with terror. Suppose, in like fashion, he pleads that he does not want to see a professional therapist, that he has confidence only in the minister, and that he will go nowhere else for help. In such a circumstance, many ministers find themselves tempted to undertake a task which may be as far beyond their personal skill as the removal of a diseased appendix. It is in such instances that an understanding of the condition and a realistic assessment of the limitation of skill or training must go hand in hand. The minister's genuine desire to help can never blind him to the fact that in certain such instances the most effective help he can provide is to enable the parishioner to seek out someone whose training has fitted him to deal responsibly with the situation. In every instance, he is sure that to offer something which he cannot produce, however well intentioned the offer might be, is to harm rather than to heal.

There is another aspect of the limitation of experience and skill which must be considered, although the principle is no different from that already set forth in the several illustrations. Sometimes it is difficult for the minister to perceive at once that his own resources may be inadequate to be of genuine help to the parishioner. The situation as described by the parishioner may sound familiar enough, and the minister may feel quite optimistic about the prospects as the interview progresses. He is not disturbed by the fact that the parishioner wishes to return at a later date to continue the exploration, and readily makes an appointment for the same hour the following week. Again, the interview goes well; certain areas are discussed which did not emerge in the initial conference, and the parishioner expresses appreciation together with a desire to return the next week at the same time. In somewhat the same fashion the pattern is repeated for a fourth, a fifth, and then a sixth interview.

Somewhere around the fifth or sixth interview the minister becomes aware of certain factors which may not have appeared before, or of which he has not been conscious. In a word, the very fact of duration is in and of itself a significant aspect of the pastoral relationship. Ordinarily it would be supposed that the kinds of stresses and strains which are the common experience of all men, and for which help is often needed when the way is rough, would be resolved in a few weeks at most. When such a resolution does not occur, then the minister raises the question within himself of whether or not he is actually being of help, and of whether or not he should continue in the interviews without some realistic assessment of where he and the parishioner are and where they seem to be going.

It should be quite clear that this kind of stocktaking does not apply to the minister's on-going relationship to the members of his parish.

Obviously he will see many of his parishioners time and time again over the course of a year as together they are involved in the various church activities. The question at issue here is the regular and sustained series of interviews following in sequence wherein the parishioner returns to continue the exploration of some personal situation or difficulty. There is a "rule of thumb" that if such a series continues into the sixth session the emotional disturbance of the parishioner is likely to be more severe than was first supposed.

Generally speaking, several rather subtle factors may begin to be operative. Without being aware of it, the pastor may be fostering a negative dependency within the parishioner. This is not to say that dependency is in and of itself always bad. There is, obviously, a sense in which every person is dependent on others to some extent, a dependency which properly varies from time to time according to the situation. Pressed too far, however, the natural dependency begins to take on negative overtones as the person becomes less and less able or willing to assume the responsibilities that are characteristic of genuine maturity. It is this kind of retreat which may be encouraged in prolonged interviews, a retreat which makes eventual resolution more difficult.

Paradoxically, as the pastor fosters negative dependency in the parishioner, he finds that he is, himself, becoming dependent on the parishioner. There is a subtle yet powerful appeal in being appreciated and sought after for help week after week. If, perchance, the pastor feels somewhat rejected by various members of his congregation, he may tend to bolster his ego by saying to himself that here is at least one person who recognizes his true worth! The minute he begins to derive such satisfaction from the recurring interviews with a parishioner, the possibility of his being any genuine help to the parishioner begins to disappear with incredible rapidity. Inevitably, he finds himself unable to maintain his own identity and integrity as he must in one form or other accede to the wishes of the parishioner in order to insure his continuation. The inevitable personal tragedy for both pastor and parishioner which follows such a relationship attests to the treachery of becoming emotionally involved beyond the realistic limits of one's own resources.

It is difficult to write these words without sounding like an alarmist. Of course it is patently true that many ministers have in fact seen parishioners over periods longer than six interviews with positive results. Yet the danger exists, nonetheless; and the recollection of ministers whose lives have been shattered by experiences which under ordinary circumstances they would have found completely foreign makes it necessary to raise the issue. There is no suggestion here that referral is always the only proper course for the minister at the conclusion of the fifth or sixth interview. Nevertheless, such a point becomes an optimum time for a realistic assessment of the situation, an assessment which may well include a consultation with someone whose professional competence equips him to assist in determining whether or not there are negative factors at work which raise danger signals or whether it seems reasonable to expect that continued interviews will likely be helpful for the parishioner. We shall consider the procedure for this kind of consultation and possible referral in a later discussion.

3. Limitation of emotional security. Thus far we have been describing the situations where the pastor finds referral indicated in terms of his own limitations—the limitation of time and the limitation of experience and skill. At every point it has been evident that the circumstance of the parishioner was crucial in making the assessment; at the same time, the discussion has focused on the minister's understanding of himself in response to the parishioner's situation as the most responsible procedure for arriving at a decision of whether or not to refer.

It was comparatively easy to see the factors involved in the limitation of time, although it was impossible to lay down any hard and fast rules to be followed. It was more difficult to define in any meaningful sense the limitation of experience or skill, although it was possible to set forth the general principles in various extreme forms. The most difficult of all to describe is the limitation of emotional security.

To begin with, it is likely that this is not the best term to employ; yet, to date, no other has appeared which gives promise of being any better. For several years in seminars with students and parish ministers I have enlisted their help in the search for a word or phrase which has a comparable clarity to "time" and "skill." One group suggested "emotional quotient" or "E.Q." borrowing the well-known "I.Q." formula. Another proposed "emotional stability." Still another, "emotional reserve." The list could run on, but the results are not impressive. Perhaps, however, the very listing suggests the idea. What is meant is the minister's freedom from emotional tensions such as threat, anxiety, fear, insecurity, loneliness, and the like. It is, of course, obvious that any such notion is always relative. Inevitably, it changes from time to time and from situation to situation.

Limitation of emotional security manifests itself in a variety of ways. In every instance, its presence can best be assessed by the minister himself, although at times it is so pronounced as to be obvious to others. A description of some of the most characteristic patterns in which the minister is handicapped by lack of emotional security may be useful in clarifying what is meant by this term.

One form of such limitation is illustrated in the interview between the student and the parishioner outside the chapel. The student reported that he was caught "flat-footed" and found himself quite uneasy by reason of the behavior of the man. There is, of course, an overlapping here with the notion of limitation of skill or experience. Nevertheless, the point at issue is that the student found himself caught in such emotional tension that it was necessary for him to devote his energies and attention toward resolving his own feelings. It is, of course, not uncommon to experience uneasiness or apprehension in the presence of the unknown or the unexpected. Indeed, such inner response is an inevitable aspect of the minister's taking seriously the plight of the parishioner and indicates his involvement in it. Thus, the question does not turn on the presence or absence of personal feeling but the extent to which such feeling becomes strong enough to distract the minister from concentrating on the parishioner. Whenever this point is reached, the minister is unlikely to be of much help, and referral is indicated.

Another occasion where limitation of emotional security tends to become crucial results when the parishioner presents a problem or describes an experience which the minister has never resolved in his

own life. Illustrations could be multiplied and would be as varied as
the lives of any given group of people. For example, the minister who
has never been able to work through feelings of resentment toward
what seemed to him to be tyrannical or authoritarian attitudes of his
father but who felt guilty by reason of his resentment would be hard
pressed to help a parishioner whose presenting problem was hostility
toward his parents. Again, the minister whose understanding of sex
was a mixture of puritanical prudery and morbid fascination would
find it difficult to listen to the tangled struggle of a teen-ager or the
agonized confession of an unfaithful wife. Again, the minister who
found himself unable to resolve certain recurring tensions in his own
marriage would likely be less than helpful when a couple in his
parish described their own frustrations in the same areas. Still again,
the minister whose work consistently suffered by reason of procrastination would probably encounter severe obstacles in responding
therapeutically to someone suffering from the same distress.

It is, of course, neither possible nor necessary for the minister to
attain a perfection in all areas of life. Indeed, it is his very participation in the varied struggles of human existence which enable him to
identify with those who find themselves overwhelmed by this or that
distress. The point, however, is that until the minister has effected
some kind of general resolution of any particular aspect of his life, he
will find himself drawn to dealing with his own feelings rather than
those of his parishioner; and in such a situation, the only promising
procedure is referral.

Still another illustration of the limitation of emotional security
appears in the instance when the minister is undergoing considerable
stress and strain in his own life. The tension might be caused by
vocational difficulties, by financial burdens, by family tensions, by
personal anxieties, or whatever. Such a situation can be short-lived or
it can be prolonged. Whatever its duration, it is evident that while
the minister is suffering from intense inner pressure, it is impossible
for him to bear part of the burden of his parishioners. In a literal
sense, the minute he attempts to assume part of the load of another,
he finds himself crushed beneath the extra weight.

The truth of this principle was made quite clear to me several years ago when a minister whom I knew quite well found himself under considerable personal pressure. In attempting to be a pastor to the members of his parish he had sufficient time and experience and skill. Yet, during the period of intense personal turmoil, he found it impossible to deal creatively with the problems through which his parishioners were passing. Since he was quite conscientious, he drove himself to carry on as usual. But the results were disastrous. Rather than being able to bear part of the burden of his parishioners, he inadvertently added to their burden since they were filled with feelings of guilt when they saw how he was literally overwhelmed by their distresses.

From another perspective, the limitation of emotional security is evident when the minister, for whatever reason, feels that his own status with some significant person is at stake in the counseling situation. Illustrations, recognizable by every clergyman, come readily to mind. Perhaps the most obvious is a situation in which an influential member of the official Church Board plays an important part. It matters little whether the presenting distress is his own or one in which he has a personal stake such as a member of his family, an employee in his business, or a friend sent by him to the minister. As long as the minister feels the necessity to "prove" himself or to behave in certain ways or to produce certain results, then it is quite unlikely that he will be able to help the individual who sits before him.

A similar condition could result from any person whose approval the minister felt essential for his own self-esteem. Thus, referral to him by a local medical doctor, by a friend, by a fellow minister might place an intolerable burden upon him. As soon as he found himself worrying about what this or that person would think regarding the outcome of the pastoral interviews, he would be generally unable to allow the person the kind of freedom which alone makes life and healing possible. Let it be clear that nothing here is meant to imply that the minister should not be sensitive to the feelings of those concerned with the parishioner, at whatever level, such as member of the family, friend, employer, and the like. The point, however, is that this concern is always balanced by a concern for the person, and at no time can his own feelings of threat be of such strength that he will be tempted to "produce" a certain outcome from the pastoral interviews. To state the matter in another way, whenever the minister finds himself thinking more of what someone else will feel about the interviews than what is happening to the parishioner, he knows that the odds are against his being of much help.

Closely related to the above is the situation wherein the minister is unable to risk failure. In such an instance, his "image" of himself is that of one who is able to "cure" everyone who comes to him. Being basically insecure, he seeks security in the reputation of being a miracle worker. Thus, he finds himself using all manner of devices to produce the kinds of outcomes which will be consistent with his image of himself.

Once again, nothing here is designed to imply that the minister should be insensitive to success or failure. Precisely because he is genuinely concerned for his parishioners, he will bend every effort to enable them to live creatively. Yet, when the time comes that he is unable to tolerate the fact of contrary choice, it is inevitable that his ability to help has been greatly impaired.

We began this section by pointing out the difficulty in finding the correct term to describe or denote the minister's limitation of emotional security. It is now apparent that this is only a part of the difficulty in dealing constructively with this factor. More than the limitation of time or skill, the limitation of emotional security is exceedingly hard for the minister to recognize. It is one thing for him to admit that he doesn't have sufficient time to see a person who is going to require prolonged therapy, but it is something else again for him to acknowledge that he would be personally unable to do so even if the time were available. Similarly, it is not too disturbing to recognize the limitation of skill—to recognize that there are those whose training and experience have better fitted them to deal with this or that trouble than is true for him. But it is quite another matter to confess that he has the time and the skill, but is personally incapacitated. For this reason, it is unfortunately probable that just at the time the minister is most beset by limitation of emotional security, he will find it necessary to resist any notion of referral. For here referral is seen as a personal defeat, as an admission of weakness, as a confession of failure. It is in this sense that a realistic recognition of the limitation of emotional security may, in fact, be the key to successful referral.

CHAPTER—3
How To Refer

Thus far we have focused attention on the factors which indicate that referral is necessary, noting in every case that the minister's own limitation whether of time, skill, or emotional stability is the key to the decision. Throughout the discussion, it has been apparent that as important as this decision is, it is only the first step in the process. Indeed, many pastors tend to feel that they are fairly adept in determining when it is proper to refer a parishioner to someone else; their problem is in not knowing how or where. It is to a consideration of these two factors we now turn in this chapter and in the one following.

There is a sense in which the first step in knowing how to refer depends upon the pastor's understanding of where to refer. From that point of view, this chapter and the next could have been reversed. The fact is, however, that there is no true sequential priority since each aspect of referral is dependent on the other. It is sufficient for now to say that the minister has the responsibility of acquainting himself with professional persons and agencies in his area so that he will be prepared when the situation calling for referral arises.

Before discussing the process of referral, it should be noted that in many instances the only thing involved is a simple providing of information regarding some group or agency which exists to meet a particular need. There is no "problem" in the sense that the parishioner is hesitant to avail himself of such resources. On the contrary he knows what is wrong and is eager to find the help that is required. On such occasions the pastor faces no difficulty other than working with the parishioner to search out the proper resource. On other occasions, however, the process is by no means so simple. The very fact of seeking help is itself the issue. In such instances the task of the pastor involves not only a knowledge of what is available, but also the enabling of the parishioner to seek such help. It is, therefore, the latter aspect which is our concern in this chapter.

Basic Principles

There are several general principles which have a direct bearing on the matter of how the referral is effected. Basic to all the rest is the minister's concern that the parishioner be helped rather than that he be perceived as the means for help. At first glance, this seems so obvious that it should require no mention. Yet, as we saw earlier, there is the constant danger that the minister will feel that if he is not able to provide the needed help then, somehow, either he or the Gospel has been found wanting. Thus, until the minister is truly convinced that his primary purpose is to do whatever is needed for the welfare of the person, either by being the primary agent for help or by being the means of getting the person to some other source of help, then his attempt at referral will be inept by definition.

When such is the attitude on the part of the minister, his next concern is that the referral be done in such a way that it is not perceived as rejection by the parishioner. This is not easy, as most ministers can testify. Ordinarily a person's decision to seek help comes after many futile attempts to resolve his problem on his own. There is a real threat to one's self-esteem to admit that he is unable to make it by himself, however much he may protest verbally that he knows everyone needs help from time to time. Once he has decided to admit his inability to another, he must also decide who the other will be. In actual fact, the process more often is exactly reversed. Through some means he comes to feel that this person (whether physician, friend, minister, or whoever) may be able to help; and, as a consequence, he approaches him with his problem. If the response he receives is a referral to someone else, he may perceive this as a denial of the trustworthiness he had thought to find and thus as an indication that help is not possible at all. To say that such a reaction is unwarranted or illogical is, of course, to miss the point—for if the person were able to function at a responsible level, he would not be seeking help in the first place. The implication, then, is that the minister needs to take particular pains to assure that the parishioner is able to see the referral for what it is—namely, the most effective help that the minister can provide and an evidence of the minister's genuine concern for his welfare.

In the third place, it is essential that the process of referral always includes the participation of the parishioner as well as the intervention of the minister. By definition the minister is taking the responsibility for suggesting an alternative course of action than that proposed by the parishioner. Inevitably there is the temptation to assume complete responsibility and thus deprive the parishioner of his own involvement in the continued therapy. It is, of course, obvious that the parishioner is unable to resolve his situation on his own, else he would not be seeking help. The danger is that the minister will overlook the necessity of enabling the parishioner to participate to the extent possible for him. While there is no rigid guideline for this relationship, the principle is clear enough. The minister assumes only that function or responsibility which the parishioner is unable to undertake, and continually reassesses the situation so that his overt involvement can decrease as the parishioner's involvement increases.

This leads to the next principle which relates to the minister's continual involvement in the referral alongside the additional person or persons who are now engaged in helping the parishioner. This does not mean that the minister will in any sense attempt to usurp the position or function of the person to whom the referral is made, or that he will in any sense engage in a jealous guarding of his own prerogatives. It does mean that the help which is now being received is in addition to rather than in place of what the minister is able to do. In essence, his function remains the same, although the outward form may vary in the light of the new relationship. This principle can be easily illustrated in the event that a parishioner requires surgery. The minister does not cease to be concerned for his welfare, but he does not attempt an operation. Moreover, there will be times when he cannot visit with his parishioner or when his visits will of necessity be quite brief and of a different character than those prior to the surgery. Throughout, however, his concern is unchanged as he searches for the means which most effectively express his genuine participation as a part of the healing team. This obvious illustration seems to become somewhat obscure when the referral is to a psychiatrist or a social agency such as The Family Service Society. For many ministers the redefinition of form or means seems to imply a denial of concern or a distortion of function. The crucial factor is the minister's own awareness of his continual involvement in the recovery of the parishioner. Once this is clear, the procedure for enabling the parishioner to perceive it follows much more readily.

Finally, there is the fact that the minister's relationship with the parishioner will continue beyond the point where the therapy received from the referral source has been completed. This, of course, is one of the great assets of the ministry, in that it provides a constant access to the parishioner in all circumstances of life rather than only in time of crisis or distress. Just as the minister does not need to await the summons of the parishioner but may take the initiative in going to offer help, so he is assured that if for any reason the expected help from the referral source did not materialize, he has the opportunity to work with the parishioner in searching elsewhere for that which is needed. It is this on-going relationship which makes essential the minister's careful attention to the process of referral in order that he not jeopardize his continued opportunity for pastoral care.

However clear the principles, the procedure in actual situations is not always as evident. As any minister can document, the pitfalls along the path of referral are as numerous as they are varied. In the illustrations which follow, we will consider the implications of the principles in particular situations.

When the Parishioner Wants Help

Undoubtedly, the easiest referral to effect is the one in which the parishioner recognizes his need for help and is ready to undertake whatever is necessary to receive it. This was the circumstance involving the alcoholic described in Chapter One. When, at last, he had poured out all the pent up hostility and bitterness, the door for referral was open. Even so, there were still obstacles. The following excerpt begins at the conclusion of the thirty-minute tirade.

1. *Parishioner:* O God, Reverend. I'm in awful shape. Is there anything you can do? Can you help me?

2. *Pastor:* I think so. At least I'm sure ready to try. I guess you're saying that you've really reached the end of your rope—that you realize now you can't go it alone.

3. *Parishioner:* That's right. What do you think I ought to do?

4. *Pastor:* Well, I think you've already done something—you've admitted that you need help. I know it's been hard to get this far. It's going to keep on being hard, for a while, anyway. But you're right far down the road. I think we ought to call the fellows from AA. They're pretty good at helping once you're ready.

5. *Parishioner:* O.K., if you say so. I been up there before and it didn't do me any good. But I'll go back if that's what you think is right. I got to do something!

6. *Pastor:* The way I see it is that when you went up there before you weren't really ready; you were just playing at it. Now, however, I think you're ready to go all out. As I said, it's going to be tough, but not really as tough as what you've already been through. And I'll stick with you no matter what.

7. *Parishioner:* O.K., Reverend. You go ahead and call them anytime you want to.

8. *Pastor:* Well, I think it'd be better if you called them. I'll look up the number for you. But let's get some breakfast first. It's still pretty early—if you want to get in the shower, I'll make up another pot of coffee.

Paradoxically, enough, the primary danger here is that the referral is too easy. Not infrequently a parishioner will profess his complete inability to do anything and implore the pastor to take over the control of his life. This relinquishing of personal responsibility is clearly illustrated in Nos. 1, 3, and 5. The minister realized that until the parishioner could honestly admit his need for help there would be little possibility of his recovery. It is evident in No. 2 that he felt the need to be sure that this was in fact the situation. His response at No. 4 could probably have been worded better, but in principle it was an attempt to affirm the dual factors of help being available and the parishioner's necessity to participate in the help. The danger of negative dependency can be seen in the first and third sentences of No. 5. At the same time, there is at least some indication of the parishioner's awareness of his own involvement in the process. In No. 6, the pastor refuses to assume the prerogative of taking full responsibility for the decision even as he does not attempt to avoid his own involvement in it. In the final sentence, he attempts to clarify his role as that of standing with the parishioner rather than of attempting to undertake the therapy for him. No. 8 is simply the overt manifestation of his genuine willingness to help together with his concern that the parishioner participate in the process to the full extent of his ability.

When Help Is Seen as Changing Others

Referral is more difficult when the person desires help, but does not see this help as involving himself. Thus, the student whose situation was described in Chapter One obviously desired to enlist the pastor's assistance, but felt that the locus of the problem was in the behavior of members of his class rather than in himself. The following excerpt indicates the thrust of the pastor's response.

1. *Student:* So I just wanted you to know why I was doing it.

2. *Pastor:* I'm glad you called me. Seems to me you're saying you just can't take any more. . . .

3. *Student:* I don't see why they do it. I've not done anything to them. If they'd just let me alone, I'd be willing to let them alone.

4. *Pastor:* (All this while I'd been attempting to devise some procedure that would be agreeable to the student but would prevent the kind of violent action I believed he would follow. I may have been unduly alarmed, but I was convinced he was capable of bodily harm to one or more of his classmates.) I see what you mean. Will you wait here just a minute while I try to check up on what we can do to work this out.

5. *Student:* Well, O.K. But you won't be gone long, will you?

6. *Pastor:* No. Only a minute, really. You wait in the Library just where you were, and I'll be right back. (At this point I felt it was necessary to run the risk of his leaving in order to check with the school authorities. I went to the phone and, fortunately, found the Dean in his office. He reported that he had been worried about this student, but had had no reason to "move in" to his situation. He agreed that psychiatric help seemed to be needed and suggested that, since the student had called me, I attempt to get him to see the psychiatrist who was the regular school consultant. I agreed and checked to make sure the psychiatrist was available. Thereafter I went back to the Reading Room where, to my relief, the student was still waiting.) Sorry to be so long. I guess you wondered whether or not I'd be back.

7. *Student:* No, I knew you'd come.

8. *Pastor:* You know, the more I've thought about this, the more it seems to me that you are really having a rough time of it. I'm not at all sure I know what's right to do, but I have a friend who may be able to help us. I know he's been of help to other students who were having difficulties, and I'd like for us to go together to see what he would suggest.

9. *Student:* Well, if you think he could help, I'd be glad to see him.

10. *Pastor:* Then, let's go. He's in his office right now, and we can go right down.

11. *Student:* All right. I'm ready.

As it turned out, the student was quite willing to go with the pastor. It is not clear whether his willingness would have been so evident if the pastor had told him that they were going to consult a psychiatrist. On the contrary, it is quite likely that his agreement signified a belief that the person to whom they were going would be prepared to intervene in the behavior of the other students. In discussing the case later, the pastor acknowledged his willingness to run the risk of communicating something other to the student than that which was in fact about to happen. His justification was that the psychiatric help was most surely needed, and that he did not want to jeopardize their going by raising the possible barrier of suggesting a visit to a psychiatrist. As a consequence of this general decision, the minister did not actually come clean with the student. What he said was correct as far as it went; it was what he left unsaid that made the difference between complete honesty and possible subterfuge.

It is comparatively simple to say that the minister has a responsibility to deal honestly with every parishioner no matter what the situation. It is not so simple to define what is meant by the term "complete honesty." If it means specific verbalization of all aspects of the situation on the part of the minister, then the matter is fairly clear. If, however, it means taking into account what will be perceived by the parishioner, then the issue is complex, indeed. Although any attempt to take into account the perception of the parishioner in a definition of "to tell the truth" opens the door to all manner of subjective distortion, it is just as possible that a rigid adherence to verbal fact may fall as far short of the mark in its own right. It is this fact that has led to all manner of controversy regarding whether or not a patient should be told that he has cancer. If this information communicates a death sentence so that the patient literally gives up when healing is possible, then it is quite possible to say that what has been communicated is not strictly "truth" at all. If, on the other hand, the withholding of diagnostic data makes possible that patient's genuine and hopeful participation in the therapeutic process so that healing does occur, it is possible that the very withholding communicates the truth, i.e., "you can get well." From a purely objective point of view, the question cannot even be raised. The situation is either this or that with no qualifying footnotes. In the end, each minister will have to make his own decision as to what actually constitutes "telling the truth." In every instance it can be hoped that the decision is reached on the basis of the situation of the parishioner as well as in terms of his own feelings.

Whatever judgment is appropriate in terms of this thorny ethical problem, there are several aspects of the interview that deserve comment. In the first place, the pastor recognized the necessity to consult with those persons who had primary responsibility for the student. In this instance, it was the academic authorities. Under other circumstances it might be parents, spouse, legal guardian, or some other duly constituted authority. While the minister has the right to suggest a certain course of action as his own opinion subject to correction in the light of subsequent events, he is never qualified to diagnose or prescribe treatment, much less institute commitment proceedings. There are not a few ministers who can testify to this fact, having found themselves involved in lawsuits as a consequence of assuming prerogatives not rightfully theirs. The point is that not all attempts to help are recognized as such by the persons involved, including the family of the parishioner who has appealed to the minister. Indeed, as we shall see later, the family of this student resented deeply his being referred to a psychiatrist and threatened to institute legal proceedings against the minister and the college for alleged defamation of character.

In the second place, the minister took time to check with the psychiatrist before suggesting this course of action to the student. While this particular procedure certainly could not be set forth as a definite rule, it implies the minister's certainty that the resource for referral which he intends to suggest is in fact available for the parishioner. In this instance, the minister was not personally acquainted with the school psychiatrist, hence the telephone call. In other instances his prior relationship to a physician or agency could be such that a particular call at the time of referral would be unnecessary. The point is that the process of referral is impeded if the parishioner comes to the decision to entrust himself to someone else, only to discover that the door is closed to him.

In the third place, the minister arranged to go with the student rather than to send him to the psychiatrist. Of course, in this situation it is likely that without someone to take him, the student would never have made it to the doctor's office. In other instances, this kind of physical accompaniment would not be as necessary. Thus, in the previous case of the alcoholic, the minister attempted to communicate the same involvement verbally by stating his intention to stand with the parishioner throughout the rough places ahead and behaviorally by looking up the proper telephone number for him. Whatever the appropriate means, the basic purpose is essential. The issue involves a clear indication that the minister is an active participant in the process of referral, is concerned that the proper help be found, and in no sense is going to wash his hands of the matter once other arrangements have been made.

The fact that the referral went smoothly is no indication that problems would not arise. As already indicated, the family of the student deeply resented the course of action followed. In like manner, the minister realized that in all probability the student might come to feel that he, too, was against him. But these were risks he was prepared to take precisely because of his concern for the welfare of the student.

When Help Is Not Seen as Personal

Even more difficult than the situation involving the alcoholic or the student is the instance where the person sees that something is needed but does not identify himself as the person in need. This circumstance is clearly illustrated in the case of the seminarian who was met by the parishioner outside the door of the Chapel. (Cf. p.. 43.) This person has no doubt that things were wrong but he saw himself as one who could provide the cure rather than as one requiring a cure. To review, the final two responses were as follows:

15. *Student:* Jack, when you see Reverend Williams, talk this over with him. Perhaps he may be able to offer some suggestions which would be of help to you.

16. *Jack:* Oh, I already have. (At this point it was time to go into the Chapel and begin the service, thankfully.)

We have already seen that the student was so unnerved by the parishioner that his only thought was to get rid of him as soon as possible. Under such circumstances his suggestion that the parishioner see the regular minister could be termed a referral only in the most general sense of the word. In one way or other every principle set forth at the beginning of this chapter was disregarded. Let it be said that these comments are not intended as a criticism of the student since he was, in fact, doing everything within his power at the time. Even so, a realistic evaluation of what happened can serve to indicate both negatively and positively what might have happened if the student had been able to respond more constructively.

In the first place, it would have been helpful if he could have sat down with the parishioner, either then or later, in order to listen more attentively to what he had to say. Quite apart from his own uneasiness, he was understandably distracted by reason of the worship service which he had to conduct in a very few minutes. Most ministers agree that they are least able to concentrate on what is being said to them immediately before or after conducting worship. It is for this reason that many ministers have attempted to devise some means for noting the comments and statements made by parishioners as they leave the Sanctuary following a service, so that they can follow up on what would otherwise probably be lost. In the illustration of the seminarian, it might have been possible to arrange a meeting in the study after the people had gone. During such an interview there would at least be an opportunity to establish a more positive relationship, on the basis of which a responsible referral might have been made.

Obviously, it is impossible to speculate very far on what might have happened in this situation had the student's response been more sound. Nevertheless, it is certain that the referral would have had a much better chance to succeed had the student suggested that he would go with the parishioner in No. 15 rather than simply suggest that he see the minister. As it stands, the suggestion is patently a move to get rid of the parishioner as quickly as possible, although the guise is referral. That the suggestion was obviously ill-timed and ill-conceived is indicated by the parishioner's response in No. 16. At that point, there is nothing for the student to do but rejoice that he has been rescued by the hands of the clock.

When Referral Is Resisted

From a somewhat different perspective there is the situation involving the person who senses the need for help but resists referral for any one of a variety of reasons. In the following excerpt, the overt resistance to psychiatric help is financial. The minister who prepared this case study indicated that the parishioner had been married for nearly fifteen years and throughout much of that time had been at odds with his wife. He had changed jobs frequently, had a tendency toward violent outbursts of temper, and on several occasions had engaged in extramarital affairs. Over a period of several years the minister had come to know both the parishioner and his wife, and had been involved in helping to straighten out several tangled situations in the home. During the time immediately prior to the interview from which this excerpt is taken events seemed to have gone from bad to worse. It was during this time that the minister became convinced that other professional help would be needed. He reported that he had suggested as much to both parties. The form of the suggestion was not reported. In the first part of the interview the parishioner, Joe, spent most of his time recounting the tensions between himself and his wife, protesting that he had carried much more than his share of the responsibility but found little cooperation from her. This recital built up to his describing a particularly violent argument as can be seen in the verbatim reconstruction.

1. *Joe:* We went after each other for quite a while, and I kicked a couple of chairs across the floor and shoved her down in one. She called me a S.O.B. and some other fancy names.

2. *Minister:* I would assume from what you have told me at other times that you have sort of lost control of yourself quite often in the last year or two.

3. *Joe:* Yeah. I threw a couple of dishes in the fireplace once and busted them up pretty bad; sometimes I kick the chairs around, but not until we get in some kind of argument. On those times we've done a pretty good job of calling each other names.

4. *Minister:* Do you mean by this that you felt much better in getting these feelings off your chest?

5. *Joe:* Well, I don't know, but I did it anyway. And look here, Reverend, she throws things around, too. When she doesn't throw things she gets all moody and goes off in the car and rides around. And sometimes when she gets into one of those moods she'll go on a

spending spree. Boy! She goes crazy, buying a bunch of things we don't need and running up bills we can't pay. Why, even when she isn't mad she's liable to go out and buy expensive furniture and things like that. She doesn't take care of what she has, and then gives me hell for not making enough money to buy her all this stuff she doesn't need anyhow!

6. *Minister:* So that as you have expressed to me before, finance is still one of your main problems.

7. *Joe:* Yeah, it just keeps creeping in. She thinks all I have to do is run down to the bank and borrow the money. Why can't she realize that you just can't do that. We got so many bills right now I can't keep up with them. And she's threatening to quit that part-time job she has! She only gets a hundred bucks a month, but I don't know what we'd do without it. It takes all that to make the payments on the stuff we already bought when we could have gotten by on something much cheaper. She's the one that needs to go to a psychiatrist!

8. *Minister:* What makes you express it that way?

9. *Joe:* She said you told her I needed to go to a psychiatrist.

10. *Minister:* She did? As you already know, Joe, we have both talked about the possibility of both of you getting help from a more professional source in order to get at some of your basic feelings and needs.

11. *Joe:* Yes, I know we have talked about this before a time or two, but I feel we ought to be able to work it out without a psychiatrist. And anyway, we can't afford it. How could we pay a psychiatrist with all the other bills we can't pay.

12. *Minister:* Certainly you would have to work this out with your wife. But if this would help to save your family and help you to live under less tension, it would be worth your considering. We are fortunate at this particular time in having a psychiatrist who comes to the County Seat twice a week for appointments. I would be happy to assist you in any way I could in considering conferences with him for both of you.

13. *Joe:* But I feel we still should be able to work this out ourselves if she would just quit nagging me all the time about my job

and about the past. I think her temper is worse than mine. If she would just let me alone when I want to sleep and when I want to help my brother.

14. *Minister:* It sounds like you just keep going over and over the same things all the time when you try to talk to each other. Well, I know you must leave now as it is time for you to go to work. Suppose we get together again in a couple of weeks.

15. *Joe:* It's all right with me. How about the same hour?

16. *Minister:* That would be fine, and in the meantime you think about the strength of the possibility of further help.

17. *Joe:* O.K. I will. But I still don't see how we can pay for anything more.

Here, again, it is not our purpose to comment on the general counseling procedure throughout the interview, although it is apparent that the minister found it difficult to deal with the harsh negative feelings being expressed. Indeed, it can be said that this inability is in and of itself sufficient indication that referral is necessary. When at last the possibility of consulting a psychiatrist does enter the conversation, the minister finds himself on the defensive and strikes back with the challenging question of No. 8. His response at No. 10 is a bit more controlled, but both here and at No. 12 he is limited to explaining his position and apparently is able to make no move toward dealing with the deeper issues involved in the parishioner's resistance. At No. 14 he gives up for the time being in the hope that the passage of time will somehow serve to weight the balance toward referral. Throughout, as he indicated in discussing the situation later, the minister was conscious of his own inability to be of help; yet, at the same time, he felt helpless in getting these persons to see someone else.

This report raises many issues, not all of which bear directly on the question of referral. For that reason, certain aspects of it will not be specifically included in the discussion although inevitably they form a part of the general picture. In the first place, this situation clearly demonstrates that all difficulties have antecedents, roots that go back far beyond the presenting difficulty. As is often the case, the persons

involved had a tendency to do as little as possible about their distresses, expending only as much time and energy as seemed to be
needed to smooth over the roughest edges. However shortsighted
such a behavior, it is certainly not uncommon. Just as a person may
take a pain-killer for a recurring toothache rather than go to the
dentist or may continue to apply superficial medication to a persistent
lesion rather than go for a medical diagnosis, so also in difficulties not
primarily physical there is often a resistance to facing up to the whole
scope of the matter. The reasons advanced for postponing what
would otherwise be considered appropriate action are usually ra-
tionalizations supported by just enough fact to make them plausible.
The person may tell himself that he is too busy just now and could
not spare the time for prolonged treatment; he may attempt to
reassure himself by noting that he is certainly not an alarmist and
need not go running to a doctor with every ache or pain; he may
profess that his financial condition is such that he cannot afford the
treatment just at this time. The list could be endless, but the end
result is the same.

Ordinarily the only means for breaking out of such a rationalizing
pattern is the experiencing of sufficient discomfort with the persistent
distress that the resistance toward overt action is overcome by the fact
that it is now more painful to do nothing. This condition is the one
described by Alcoholics Anonymous who say that the person must
"hit bottom" before he is ready to do anything significant about his
drinking problem. In like manner, when the pain from the tooth
becomes unbearable, the fear of going to the dentist is tipped in the
balance to the lesser of the two evils; or when the extent of the lesion
continues to expand despite the frequent application of medication,
the hesitation to go to the doctor is overcome by the fear of further
procrastination.

In the light of this common, if illogical, condition the task of the
pastor in dealing with the distresses of his people becomes complex,
indeed. The crucial question turns on how far he is justified in
continuing to "help" his parishioners, if his efforts are primarily
serving the purpose of reducing their distress to the degree that they
can avoid for a while longer seeking the kind of therapy which they

require. In the previously described situation with the married couple, there is every evidence that this danger exists. The pastor reported that over a period of several years he had been involved with the couple helping to straighten out recurring distresses. At some point and moment it is necessary to evaluate what is happening over the long haul lest, to put the matter quite crassly, his pastoral attentions actually result in becoming a kind of emotional "aspirin tablet."

The issue is much easier to state than to practice. It is certainly true that all life fluctuates between joy and sorrow, success and defeat, love and hate. It is also true that no man lives or dies to himself, and that at many points there is need for someone to help bear the burdens which have become momentarily too great to be borne alone. In most instances the steadying hand and the shifting of the load prove sufficient for the person to go on his own—now, once again, able to cope with the circumstances with which he has to strive. The help he receives is genuine, and the restitution is realistic. And if, on certain occasions, there is a glossing over of some aspect or facet of the difficulty, it is certain that another time will come when opportunity is given to deal with that, also. Unresolved areas of one's life cannot be ignored for prolonged periods of time. The danger comes in following any course of action which accomplishes nothing more than to obscure the warning signals.

When at length, by whatever criterion, the minister concludes that what he is doing falls into the category of postponing rather than providing help, he moves toward referral. This was the situation in the previously described pastoral report on the married couple. Thus, the problem was not so much *whether* to refer as it was *how* to refer, a problem complicated by the parishioner's resistance to any suggestion of the idea. As has already been noted, the pastor felt himself unable to be of any substantial benefit to these persons but at the same time helpless in enabling them to see someone else. Caught on the horns of this dilemma, he followed what seemed to be the line of least resistance, that of continuing to see them himself hoping against hope that somehow the way would open up for them to go to the psychiatrist.

From one point of view, it could be said that in this situation the pastor's problem was not lack of knowledge but inability to act on the knowledge he already had. It is certain that he found himself manipulated by these parishioners who stated that if he did not see them there would be no one to help. In the seminar discussion where the case was presented, he described his own feeling as being unable to "cast them adrift" since it was "obvious that they needed help so badly." He further stated that he wasn't absolutely sure that the psychiatrist could help them in their present state of resistance and, thus, concluded that what little help he was able to give was better than no help at all.

Understandably, the other ministers in the seminar found themselves very much in sympathy with this position, recognizing its similarity to experiences in their own pastoral care. While it was comparatively simple to spell out the principle by using, as we did earlier, the analogy of a person imploring the pastor to perform an appendectomy, they were properly insistent that the analogy was just that and noted that somewhere along the way the similarity broke down.

At length the discussion turned to the exploration of what might be considered positive as well as negative aspects of the pastor's continuing to see the parishioners under such circumstances. It became evident that two factors were of prime importance. In the first place, there was the necessity that the pastor be quite clear as to the realistic definition of himself in the on-going process as one who might be of help in enabling the parishioner to work through his resistance to the referral—but in no sense as one who intended to be the sole means of help, apart from some additional resource. It was recognized that resistance to referral, however ill-founded, may be nonetheless real in the life of the parishioner. In that instance, the pastor performs a genuine and necessary ministry as he stands with the parishioner in the threatening prospect of taking a step which is fearful and unknown.

In the second place, there was the necessity for the minister to terminate the interviews if it became clear that their continuation was proving a hindrance rather than a help toward referral. Although such a decision would be reached only after agonizing assessment which, literally, left no stone unturned in giving the parishioner the benefit of the doubt, there was no question that for the minister to be of help the possibility, and at times the actuality, of such a procedure had to be faced.

In the discussion, it turned out that the extremes could be stated with a fair amount of certainty. On the one hand there would be times when the minister would terminate the interviews too quickly, not recognizing that after only one or two more times the person would be able to seek further help. On the other hand, there would be times when the minister would continue the interviews too long, not recognizing that each successive appointment reduced the possibility for genuine help to be received when, if ever, it was sought. As would be expected, each minister present wished for a definite rule or measure which would tell precisely when he should do what. And, as every minister realizes, no such device exists.

Throughout the consideration of this aspect of referral, it has been increasingly evident that the "when" and the "how" factors are inextricably bound together. As we have already noted, it can be argued that the minister's difficulty was not so much an unawareness of procedure as an indecision regarding whether to put into practice what he knew. However valid the argument, we have considered this interview under the "how" section for the simple reason that the minister reports that he had, in fact, decided that referral was needed. Taken at face value, this statement is sufficient to focus attention on how he could proceed in the light of this decision.

The principle, as indicated above, includes his realistic definition of himself together with his genuine concern for the parishioner's struggle in the context of this definition. Although it is highly questionable to project a conversation which could conceivably take place because, in fact, there is no way of knowing how the parishioner will respond, the following hypothetical excerpt may serve to illustrate the principle in actual practice. Since any such fabricated beginning is synthetic at best, we will take up the interview at No. 10.

10. *Minister:* I don't remember saying it just that way. As you know, Joe, I did say to both of you that I believe you need more help than I can give. I guess you're saying it seemed I was really aiming this at you.

11. *Joe:* Yeah. To tell the truth, it did. Look, Reverend, I feel we ought to be able to work this out without a psychiatrist. And anyway,

we couldn't afford it. How could we pay a psychiatrist with all the other bills we can't pay?

12. *Minister:* I guess you're saying that right now it seems impossible, and that anyhow you'd like to think you could get by without having to do it.

13. *Joe:* Yeah. I sure do wish we could. Boy, when I think about going to see a psychiatrist, it gives me the shakes. Can't you just keep on seeing us, Reverend. You've helped us an awful lot in these past few years.

14. *Minister:* No, I don't believe so, Joe. I really want you all to get this worked out, and I'm afraid if I keep on seeing you it won't be enough. If I get you right, however, you'd sure rather keep on with me than go somewhere else.

15. *Joe:* You can say that again. Why don't you think you can keep on helping us?

16. *Minister:* Well, Joe, it's just that I've done all I can, and things seem to be getting worse, not better. Let me say that if you decide to go to the psychiatrist, it's not like I was going to desert you. You know I'll be with you all the time just like now. It's just that I feel you need more help than I can give you, and my main concern is that you get straightened out. By the way you ask, I guess you're saying it seems a little strange that I would suggest this now.

17. *Joe:* Yeah. Gee, I don't know, Reverend. When you put it that way, I think I see what you mean. But, gosh! Going to see a psychiatrist!

18. *Minister:* Sort of bugs you to think about it.

19. *Joe:* Sure does. (pause) Let me turn it over in my mind for a while. Gee, I don't know. . . .

20. *Minister:* O.K. I guess you're saying that it'll take a little getting used to before you can make up your mind. I'd be glad to see you at this time next week, and we could see how it stands.

21. *Joe:* All right. (pause) O.K. That sounds O.K. to me. And thank you. It's sort of rugged to think of going to somebody else.

Although this excerpt is admittedly fabricated, it is nonetheless based on fact in that it follows the pattern which has been observed in many such instances. What is noteworthy is that at every response the minister attempted to define his perception of the situation, while at the same time demonstrating his understanding of the parishioner's point of view and his acceptance of him as he wrestled with the threatening prospect of seeing a psychiatrist. Nowhere did the minister deny or obscure his own integrity nor retreat from his conviction that additional help should be sought. At the same time, he continually manifested his willingness to stand with the parishioner despite the fact that their viewpoints differed quite widely. It is certainly not the intention of this suggested procedure to give the impression that if such a format is followed, the result will inevitably be positive. At the same time, it is certain that only through some such procedure as this is a constructive and helpful outcome possible.

When the Interviews Continue

The final aspect of our discussion of the process of referral deals with the responsibility of the minister at the conclusion of the fifth or sixth interview. In the previous chapter we noted that the necessity for referral may not appear at first, nor may it be readily apparent in the material being presented by the parishioner. Nevertheless, the very duration of any particular series of interviews is in and of itself sufficient indication of deeper inner tension to cause the minister to raise the question of whether more help is needed—more than he is able to provide.

Although not basically different in principle from the illustration discussed in the previous section, there are certain variations which require additional comments. In the first place, there may be no overt manifestations to which the pastor could point as indications that all was not going well. In the previous illustration, the parishioner continued to experience violent outbursts of temper and found himself at almost perpetual odds with his wife. Conceivably, in the matter of number of interviews, the parishioner might seem to be making progress and honestly report that things were, on the whole, somewhat better—despite an occasional setback or so.

Again, there may or may not be any manifest resistance to referral. While it is entirely possible that the parishioner might voice a reluctance to seeing someone else, the presence or absence of such hesitation is not in and of itself sufficient to indicate whether or not the decision to refer is warranted. As we shall see, there are occasions when the parishioner quite readily agrees to an interview with another person only to resist any further contact, although this may seem indicated.

Still, again, the pastor may justifiably come to feel that it is proper for him to continue his interviews with the parishioner, following the session with another person. Put in other terms, the decision to seek referral at this juncture of a pastoral relationship more closely resembles consultation than was the case in the situation described above.

In the illustration which follows it is possible to observe in an actual experience the process implied in this type of referral. The parishioner, Mrs. R., is a thirty-eight-year-old mother of two children. Her husband is a successful executive in a rather large national organization. Active in the church, Mrs. R. is capable and has been willing to undertake a variety of assignments in the Women's Organization, the Church School, and the Youth Groups. The pastor reported that his initial interview with her in this particular series was scheduled when she requested to see him "to talk over some things regarding the Church School." He frankly admitted that his expectation was that the conversation would center on some structural aspect of the educational program such as curriculum or teacher recruitment, and that he was somewhat surprised when she rather quickly moved to a recounting of some of her own tensions. Somehow, it seemed to her that she had more difficulty getting things done than before, and it worried her that she seemed to bog down in details which formerly would have presented no problem. She said she didn't really think that there was anything basically wrong with her, but that she appreciated the opportunity "just to talk it out." During the interview, she noted that she and her husband had tried to get at what was bothering her, but "he really thinks I'm making a mountain out of a molehill." It was finally the husband who suggested that she come to see the minister. "I'm sure he can help you to get these things sorted out and get back on the beam."

At the conclusion of the first interview, Mrs. R. expressed genuine appreciation for the minister's time and indicated that she felt much better although she really hadn't "reached any solution." When the minister indicated that he would be glad to see her again if she wished, she readily accepted the offer, and an appointment was made for the same hour the following week. In the second interview, she was more pensive than before. "I'm not sure I should be here taking up your time with my troubles; indeed, I'm not sure I have any right to call these things 'troubles' when I think of all the suffering in the world." As the hour progressed, she spoke of little irritations in the home. "Maybe it's just me, but the children seem to get on my nerves, and Jim doesn't seem to pay any attention to what's happening to them." At the conclusion of the interview she requested that she be allowed to return "if you can spare the time." The appointment was set for the following week.

The third interview did not differ greatly from the second, although Mrs. R. seemed even more moody than before. As she spoke of her children the irritations which had seemed somewhat trivial on the previous week seemed to loom a bit larger. She spent some time exploring her feelings about her husband and felt some guilt in the process. "He certainly is a wonderful man; good provider, and loves the children. I guess I really ought to be ashamed of myself when I talk about him that way." When the end of the hour came, she seemed to assume that she would be coming back. "Is this same time next week O.K.?"

In discussing the series of interviews later, the pastor noted that there was no major presenting symptom which in and of itself raised a danger signal. On the contrary, the kinds of distress being described by Mrs. R. seemed to be of the sort common to all people in the ordinary ventures of life. It was, in fact, precisely because there seemed to be no overt difficulty sufficient to warrant the continuing interviews that he first began to raise the question within himself as to whether he was in fact truly responding to what Mrs. R. was saying. When the same pace was followed in the fourth and fifth interviews, he became convinced that something was being overlooked.

The following excerpt occurred toward the end of the sixth interview.

1. *Mrs. R.:* . . . and that's not like me. Some days it's better than it was, but this week . . . I don't know. . . .

2. *Minister:* Sort of discouraging to you that you can't see any real progress.

3. *Mrs. R.:* Yeah, I guess so. . . . Yes, it is. Yet, as I've said before, I really have no right to complain. Jim was saying last night that there are thousands of people who would give anything to be in my shoes; and he's right!

4. *Minister:* A kind of guilty feeling that somehow you ought to count your blessings rather than look at your troubles. Yet, pretty hard to do . . .

5. *Mrs. R.:* It sure is. And I do try . . . I really try. . . .

6. *Minister:* Mrs. R., I've been thinking about what you've been saying these past few weeks, and I think I understand some of the real struggle you're having. What bothers me is that somehow things don't seem any better; indeed, maybe worse. And yet, you're trying . . . trying real hard. I think you know my real concern is that you get over this, and I hate to see it dragging along like it has. This has caused me to ask myself whether there is something here we're overlooking, something neither of us can see. It's a real possibility, I believe, although it's also possible that nothing of the kind is happening. Just to be sure, to find out one way or other, I'd like for us to check with a friend of mine, Dr. F. R. Kennington, who's had a great deal of experience in helping people in trouble. If you're willing, I'd like for you to see him one time and tell him what you've told me. If we're on the right track, then that'll be encouraging to both of us; if not, then the sooner we get there, the better.

7. *Mrs. R.:* Well uh . . . well, I really hadn't thought of . . . uh . . .

8. *Minister:* I guess you're saying this kind of caught you off base, that you're not real sure what you think. . . .

9. *Mrs. R.:* That's right. I sort of thought things were getting along pretty good, I guess. . . . Talking with you, I mean. . . . But if you think so . . .

10. *Minister:* I really do think so; but I gather it's still a kind of strange idea to you.

11. *Mrs. R.:* Yes. In a way, yes. . . . I guess I kinda hate to start all over with someone else.

12. *Minister:* I see what you mean. Actually, it won't really be starting all over, but I guess you're saying that's certainly what it looks like.

13. *Mrs. R.:* Yes, from here it does. (pause) Yet, I can see how it really isn't, I think. I'll have to talk it over with Jim, but I think he'll be for anything that will help me get hold of myself. Can I call you tomorrow?

14. *Minister:* That would be fine. If you agree, I want to talk to Dr. Kennington also, just to check my own impressions of what we're doing. As I said, it is entirely possible that we are on the right track, and that would be most gratifying to me. On the other hand, if we're overlooking something I'd sure like to know it so we could get at it right away. When you decide, let me know, and I'll help you make an appointment.

15. *Mrs. R.:* All right. I'll let you know first thing tomorrow.

There are several factors which stand out in this illustration. In the first place, the minister's statement in No. 6 is basically sound, even though it could have been improved in several ways. In essence it sets forth his honest conviction regarding the situation, his genuine concern that Mrs. R. receive proper help, and his willingness to continue the relationship either in cooperation with the psychiatrist or on his own depending on what emerged in the consultation. It is probable that the length of his statement reflected some of his own uncertainty, and in all likelihood he did not communicate to her exactly what he intended. The only identification of Dr. Kennington was "a friend of mine" who has "had a great deal of experience in helping people in trouble." Significantly, however, this does not seem to have been an issue for Mrs. R. The minister apparently realized that whatever he said would be open to misunderstanding, and was prepared to deal with whatever need for clarification seemed to emerge. In this instance, the more pressing matter came at the point of her uncertainty about "starting over." In No. 12, the minister indicated that he did not share this judgment, but that he recognized her point of view as being real for her.

In the second place, as illustrated specifically in No. 10 and No. 12, but evident throughout, the minister was able to maintain a constructive balance between setting forth his own conviction and responding to the parishioner's feelings in the light of his position. As any minister can attest, this balance is difficult to achieve. There is an almost overwhelming tendency to concentrate on the affirmation, to enlarge upon it, explain it, defend it. In so doing, there is little opportunity to continue listening to the parishioner since, by definition, there is a desire that the parishioner do the listening. The minister in this illustration was remarkably successful in avoiding such a pitfall. Thus, where he stood was made quite clear at all times; yet, throughout he demonstrated an understanding of Mrs. R.'s position and his willingness for her to deal honestly with her uncertainties, which directly included his own judgment in the matter.

In the third place, the minister told the parishioner of his intention to see the psychiatrist in conjunction with her interview. His purpose was to make clear that everything was out in the open, that he was not engaged in discussing her situation "behind her back." This raises the issue of privileged communication and the extent to which the minister is justified in consulting another professional person about a parishioner without the parishioner's knowledge. We will discuss this at great length in Chapter Five. It is sufficient for now to note that in the present illustration the minister was convinced that a strict openness was essential for any continuing relationship which he hoped to have with Mrs. R. At the same time, it is not clear just what was meant by his saying, "If you agree . . ." in No. 14. It may be taken to indicate her agreement to see the psychiatrist, herself, or it may imply her agreement that the minister do so. If the former, then the minister must still face the question of what he will do in the event that she decides not to go. Here the situation is similar to that already discussed—namely, the realistic recognition that his continuation in the relationship may be more harmful than helpful, since it provides for the parishioner a justification for not seeking more adequate help elsewhere.

As it turned out in this situation, Mrs. R. did see the psychiatrist as did the minister. On the basis of their consultation, it was decided that the minister would continue the weekly interviews with Mrs. R., and that at regular intervals he would confer with the psychiatrist on their progress. Under this arrangement the relationship extended over several months, during which time Mrs. R. worked through many previously unresolved attitudes and feelings. It seemed evident that she did receive genuine help toward living a more creative life.

Although, in the strictest sense, this illustration did not involve referral in that the minister continued to see the parishioner, the principles inherent are nevertheless the same. In a similar situation it seemed indicated that the parishioner should work with the psychiatrist rather than the minister. The decision was reached not only because it appeared that the tensions being experienced by the parishioner were quite complex, but also because the minister had serious doubts about his ability to sustain the relationship over a long period of time. He recognized, however, that the process of referral in such a situation might require more than one interview, and he was willing to see his role as that of helping the parishioner deal with his uncertainties about changing his course in what appeared to be "midstream." The following excerpt is taken from the interview which came several days following the parishioner's seeing the psychiatrist.

1. *Parishioner:* So that's how it is. He thinks I ought to come back, and even set up an appointment for me next week. But I told him I'd have to think it over. I don't know . . .

2. *Minister:* Is this to say you haven't made up your mind? You're not sure this is what you ought to do?

3. *Parishioner:* That's right. He seemed like a nice person, but . . . well . . . I guess it's just the idea of going to a psychiatrist. . . . Do you really think this is the thing for me to do?

4. *Minister:* Well, right now, yes. You know, of course, that there's no way to guarantee success; that is, he may be able to help, and he may not. But I am sure that he is a good man and that he has helped friends of mine in the past. That's why I wanted you to see him; I believe he can help you.

5. *Parishioner:* Yeah. Well, I don't know. It's just that going to a psychiatrist . . . Well, does this mean I'm . . . crazy?

6. *Minister:* Of course not! It simply means that you have run up against some things which are a little more than you can handle right now. Like when you need a doctor for the "flu" or something like that.

7. *Parishioner:* Yeah, I guess so. I'd still rather come to see you. You already know all about me, and I know you could help.

8. *Minister:* I surely hope I can help. Way I see it now, the most help I can be is to see that you work with the doctor. You know I want you to get well.

9. *Parishioner:* Yeah, I know that. But don't you think it'd be O.K. for us to keep on for a little while? I mean . . . well, maybe I'll start to work some of these things out.

10. *Minister:* John, if I thought so, I'd sure do it. But, honestly, I don't think so; and to keep on would promise you more than I could deliver.

11. *Parishioner:* Well, I'll have to think about it. It costs a lot of money, you know. And I'd like to be sure . . .

12. *Minister:* John, if you had to have an operation for appendicitis, you'd go ahead, even if it would cost a lot of money. This is sort of the same thing, in a way. In the end, it'll be money well spent, because you'll be all right again.

When contrasted with the procedure in the previous illustration, this one leaves something to be desired. It never was possible for the minister to listen openly to the hesitation of the parishioner. Rather, he felt himself pushed to defend a course of action and spent his entire time attempting to explain and justify his position. It is likely, as indicated earlier, that this defensiveness was in itself a manifestation of the minister's own uncertainty about helping the parishioner. In that sense, his decision to refer is quite sound.

Apart from actual method, however, his intention is quite good. His obvious purpose, aside from a need to justify himself, is to enable the parishioner to bring himself to the point where he can set up regular appointments with the psychiatrist. His task would have been considerably easier if, during the interview, he had been able to recognize and accept the reluctant feelings of the parishioner. As it was, his attempts to convince the parishioner of the validity of the decision probably drove a wider wedge in their relationship. In spite of this, what he did was far superior to his doing nothing and for that reason deserves a place in the "plus" column. That he could have done much more to assure his continued relationship with the parishioner is, from the standpoint of purpose, beside the point. If, at the end of the interview, the parishioner refused to go to the psychiatrist, the minister would be faced with the question of whether or not he should see him again. In line with the principle already discussed, the answer would turn on whether the reason for another interview was to help the parishioner work through his reluctance to be referred or to attempt to provide the help which otherwise would have been afforded by the psychiatrist. In the case of the former, another interview could be justified, but not in the case of the latter.

Conclusion

Throughout this discussion on how to refer, we have been assuming some reluctance on the part of the parishioner. In many instances, of course, there will be no such hesitation. Rather, the fact that the minister recognizes his limitation of whatever sort and refers the parishioner to someone who can be of genuine help is in and of itself sufficient for the step to be taken.

Even so, there is always to some extent or other the feeling on the part of the parishioner that since he came to the pastor, it is the pastor who should provide the help. In such instances, it is not always easy to see that help may be precisely the purpose of referral. It is for this reason that the principles are of primary importance, whatever the position of the parishioner. If the pastor is truly able to help the parishioner establish a relationship with the proper person, whatever his need, then he has in fact performed a genuine service.

CHAPTER—4
Where To Refer

One of the most significant factors in this century is the development of wide varieties of resources for the meeting of human ills. Through both public and private institutions and agencies, there has been a phenomenal increase in substantial efforts to provide relief from suffering and help in time of trouble. As would be suspected, the more complex problems are dealt with in areas of population concentration; but the fact of modern transportation has reduced the distance between countryside and town and has put the full range of facilities within the reach of practically everyone.

From the standpoint of the minister, whether he lives in an urban area or in a more sparsely populated rural community, the primary consideration is that he familiarize himself with the resources available to him for referral and establish some working relationship with these resources prior to the time they will be needed. While it is probably inevitable that some situation or problem will be brought to him which will require his making an investigation at the time of the request, his ordinary procedure is not only to be acquainted with the services and agencies in his area but also to know those key persons in the agencies who will be involved in the referrals. It is only from this position that he is able to know in advance the kind of help to be expected by his parishioners—and to describe with integrity the possibilities and limitations of the referral resource.

In accomplishing this purpose, there is nothing which can replace a personal call. Of course the minister will familiarize himself with the services performed by the several professions and agencies through literature and brochures, but the knowledge gained by a first-hand visit is an invaluable asset when the actual time for referral comes. It goes without saying that the minister will exercise discretion in such calls, taking care not to be a burden and remembering the busy schedule of the persons involved. Moreover, his call is not in the nature of an investigation or inquiry which is designed to render a value judgment or place the persons visited "on the spot." Rather, the minister may simply introduce himself, point out that he is new in the community, and indicate that he is desirous of discovering the kinds of services and resources available so that he may be of more help to the people who turn to him in time of need. It is also quite proper to offer himself as a resource for referral should the need arise when an individual wishes to see a clergyman and has no regular church connection in the community.

As has already been noted, on many occasions the only thing necessary for referral is the information regarding where the appropriate help may be obtained. Usually there is no particular problem involved in such procedure. For obvious reasons we have been dealing primarily with the situations where the referral itself is the occasion for tension, as well as with the matter which occasions the referral. In the listings which follow, both aspects are present, although in many instances the minister is not called upon to provide the direct information where there is no question but that referral is necessary.

There are various ways of listing resources for referral. One is to categorize the major areas of distress and then examine the particular groups or agencies which may be expected to help in each category. This, generally, is the format of a valuable book entitled *Where to Go for Help*[1] by Wayne E. Oates and Kirk H. Neely, which is a revision of Oates' book by the same name published some years ago. This volume can be used to great advantage by ministers who are faced with varying difficulties on the part of their parishioners. Despite the fact that it was not written primarily for clergymen, it has served the purposes of

1. Philadelphia, The Westminster Press, 1972.

referral for many ministers. Another scheme for listing resources available to the minister is to group the agencies and professions, indicating the scope of each. This latter is the format followed here. We will look first at the private professions, then turn to community organizations. Next we will examine some of the private organizations and finally note briefly certain religious groups and services.

It should be clearly understood that the listings included here are not intended to be exhaustive. Limitation of space precludes any complete cataloging of available services. It is hoped, however, that on the basis of this descriptive discussion the minister will be able to assess the kinds of help which exist in his area and thereby be in a better position to draw on the resources available to him and his parishioners in time of trouble.

The Private Professions

1. Medicine. A primary resource in any situation requiring extensive help is the medical doctor. Throughout the years the clergyman and the physician have represented the whole range and spectrum of the helping professions. In this day of specialization, with particular skills and procedures mastered by individuals and groups, the general practitioner still remains the one most available to the clergyman in time of distress.

It is encouraging to note the tremendous strides that have been made in recent years to provide for closer cooperation between the clergyman and physician. Ecclesiastical groups have set up committees on faith and health, and many medical associations sponsor seminars dealing with the treatment of the whole person including ways in which physicians and ministers can cooperate for the welfare of the patient. Yet, despite this progress, much remains to be done in order for the doctor and the minister to work side by side on the healing team. In recent years I have had the opportunity to meet with many groups of clergymen and physicians whose purpose in coming together was to discuss areas of cooperation. Inevitably I have found that there is a genuine cordiality in such groups manifested in protestations of friendship and good working relationships. Nevertheless, when specific questions are put, such as "When did you, as a physician, last refer a patient to a minister?" or "When did you, as a clergyman, last confer with a physician about some parishioner?" the answers tend to become quite vague. I have heard physicians say that they were very hesitant to refer a patient to a clergyman since they were not entirely sure how well his training had qualified him to deal with the distress being suffered. In addition, I have heard physicians say that their hesitation to consult with a clergyman grew out of the fact that although they received a fee for their services, the minister did not; and thus they thought it presumptuous to ask for his time.

Clergymen, on the other hand, have often expressed dismay when it seemed that hospital doors were inexplicably closed to them, or that the physician was so busy that he could not find an appropriate opportunity to confer about the condition of a parishioner, or that the physician was reluctant to help with a chronic alcoholic or an adolescent with behavior problems. At a deeper level, clergymen have at times been puzzled by what appeared to be a rift between physicians engaged in the practice of internal medicine and those engaged in the practice of psychiatry. As a consequence, these clergymen have not always been sure of what reception a parishioner would receive if referred with a difficulty which seemed to have emotional dimensions.

For some years the American Medical Association maintained a Department of Medicine and Religion which was charged with the responsibility of promoting a better working relationship between ministers and physicians. This department is no longer in existence, a fact which I regret since my experience with the work done by the department was positive. Even so, the legacy of this work is still part of the general growing cooperation between clergy and physicians, and my hope is that conversations and seminars between these two professions can go on apace. From such discussions can come the kind of mutual understanding and respect which will truly enable the minister and the doctor to join hands in helping those who suffer.

2. Psychiatry. It is historically true that psychiatry and religion have often been set over against each other. Some of the reasons for this cleavage have been apparent, some more obscure. But the fact remains that in many instances the minister has felt a real hesitation in referring a parishioner to a psychiatrist for fear that religious faith will at best be ignored, or at worst treated as a pathological symptom. As a consequence of this mistrust there have been occasions when a person was not enabled to seek psychiatric treatment at a time when the possibility of healing was greatest.

In recent years there has been an encouraging movement toward closing the gap between these two professions. Aided by groups whose purpose it has been to bring representatives of each discipline together in face-to-face dialogue, there has emerged a more responsible understanding on the part of both as to the concerns and responsibilities of the other. Hopefully such discussions will continue, for by no means have all the areas of tension been resolved.

Meanwhile, it is inevitable that psychiatrists will tend to be located in urban areas, at least in the foreseeable future. For this reason, the minister in the smaller community may not actually have much opportunity to know a psychiatrist personally. While ordinarily he will be in consultation with a local physician, he can also obtain help from the American Psychiatric Association, 1700 Eighteenth Street, N. W., Washington, D. C., 20009. This group publishes a directory of its members which is available through its publications office, $5.00 for members, $8.00 for non-members. Members are listed alphabetically and geographically according to their membership status and certifications, e.g., Psychiatry, Neurology, Child Psychiatry, etc. In addition, the central office will provide the name of the secretary of the appropriate District Branch of the Association to anyone wishing names of qualified psychiatrists in a given area. Most states have District Branches of the Association except for certain western states which have regional branches. Densely populated areas may have more than one branch. Information concerning an updated version of the APA *Biographical Directory* may be obtained by writing to R. R. Bowker, Publisher, P.O. Box 1807, Ann Arbor, Michigan 48106.

3. Psychology. In recent years the practice of counseling by qualified psychologists, who have been trained in clinical experience, has emerged as a genuine resource for referral. Nevertheless, it is necessary to note that as yet there is still considerable discrepancy in the qualifications of those who offer themselves as counselors. For this reason the minister will want to make absolutely certain that the person to whom he refers a parishioner is qualified to render the service necessary. Many state legislatures have established recognized standards for certification to do therapy on the basis of proposals from the American Psychological Association. This is not the case for all areas, and apart from such certification it remains true that persons with little or no professional training will offer their services through the classified pages of the telephone book as well as through other media of advertising.

While the American Psychological Association does not attempt to maintain a list of qualified persons, they will provide the name and address of the State Association Secretaries who can provide information regarding local psychologists who are qualified to do therapeutic counseling. The address of the APA is 1200 Seventeenth Street, N. W., Washington, D. C., 20036.

4. Clergy. Throughout the years the clergy have been a resource for fellow ministers to help with parishioners in distress. As far back as the early centuries of the Christian era certain clergymen have demonstrated by their experience that they were prepared to deal with particular situations. Only in the past few years, however, have standards for clergy who have particular skills and experience in pastoral care and counseling been established. The American Association of Pastoral Counselors, 3 West 29th Street, New York, New York 10001 publishes a directory of members who have demonstrated their competence in this area.

This listing is of value to the minister who is seeking referral resources in all parts of the country.

One of the phenomena of the mid-twentieth century is the emergence of Pastoral Counseling Centers. As would be expected, those who participate in such centers vary widely in training and experience. On occasion, ordination plus twenty hours of specialized instruction is deemed adequate for staff preparation. Other centers require far more prerequisites for inclusion at professional levels. The AAPC has to date given more attention to the certifying of members than the accreditation of centers, but that is beginning to change. It is likely that in the very near future a comprehensive listing of pastoral counseling centers that meet high standards will be available. At the present time addresses for those centers already accredited can be obtained from the AAPC address given above.

Community Organizations

The list of community organizations comprising the various welfare and social service groups has increased remarkably since World War II. In most urban centers there is some association to deal with practically every aspect of human suffering. Most often associated with the general fund-raising program of the community, these agencies are available to the minister as resources for the needs of his parishioners.

As has been noted, even the rural areas have access to most of the facilities provided by the more populous regions. The County Welfare Office serves a valuable function to the most isolated of churches. In the larger communities there is a council which serves the purpose of coordinating the various groups designed to meet human suffering. Called by a variety of names, i.e. the Community Chest, the Red Feather Agencies, the United Givers Fund, these cooperative ventures make available to the pastor a range of services which goes far beyond his own resources. Listings of the various groups and organizations can be obtained by calling the local community council or cooperative welfare office.

Many of the groups associated with the Community Chest or United Givers Fund are affiliated with national organizations. In the listings included below the addresses of national offices are given so that the minister whose community does not have a local chapter may discover the nearest group.

Informational groups.   There are certain groups which are not counseling agencies, strictly speaking. Their primary purpose is to assure appropriate standards and to disseminate information. The four organizations listed below fall into this category.

American Social Health Association.

The American Social Health Association, with home offices at 260 Sheridan Avenue, Suite 307, Palo Alto, California, 94306 (415-321-5134) is supported by the nation's united community campaigns. It maintains four regional offices throughout the country as follows:

Eastern Region: P.O. Box 30526
                Gahanna, Ohio 43230
                Phone: 614-475-2767

Connecticut	Maryland	New York
Delaware	Massachusetts	Pennsylvania
District of Columbia	New Hampshire	Rhode Island
Maine	New Jersey	Vermont

Mid-Western Region: (Operates out of the same office as the Eastern)

Illinois	Michigan	North Dakota
Indiana	Minnesota	Ohio
Iowa	Missouri	South Dakota
Kansas	Nebraska	Wisconsin

Southern Region: 100 Edgewood Ave., N.E., Room 525
Atlanta, Georgia 30303
Phone 404-522-0110 Ext. 160

Alabama	Louisiana	South Carolina
Arkansas	Mississippi	Tennessee
Canal Zone	New Mexico	Texas
Florida	North Carolina	Virginia
Georgia	Oklahoma	West Virginia
Kentucky		

Western Region: 260 Sheridan Avenue, Suite 307
Palo Alto, California 94306
Phone: 415-321-5134

Alaska	Hawaii	Oregon
Arizona	Idaho	Utah
California	Montana	Washington
Colorado	Nevada	Wyoming

Child Welfare League of America, Inc.

The Child Welfare League of America, 67 Irving Place, New York, New York, 10003 (Phone: 212-254-7410) has as its goal the improvement of services for the deprived, the neglected, the dependent children of the United States. Its services include accreditation of agencies dealing with children, research in the care and treatment of children, and informational resources through publications and conferences. A *Directory of Member Agencies* is available through the address above at $8.00 per copy including postage and handling. Payment must accompany order.

Mental Health Association.

The Mental Health Association coordinates the programs and activities of state and local associations. Among its services are informational films, publications, and conferences to assist local groups in the effecting and maintaining of mental health.

The National Headquarters are located at 1800 North Kent

Street, Arlington, Virginia 22209. In addition there are state and local organizations whose addresses may be obtained by writing to the national address.

National Council on Family Relations.

The National Council on Family Relations is not a counseling agency, but rather an organization to foster a better understanding of relationships within the home and to facilitate an awareness of those factors which make for more constructive family living. Services include the publication of the *Journal of Marriage and the Family* together with annual meetings which provide helpful experiences for ministers. The home address is 1219 University Avenue, S. E., Minneapolis, Minnesota, 55414.

Service Groups.   Among the many service groups and agencies, the five listed below indicate the kinds of resources available for the minister. By no means exhaustive, these organizations are representative of the variety of services found in most urban areas.

American Association of Marriage and Family Counselors.

The American Association of Marriage and Family Counselors is an inter-professional group of certified members whose training and experience have qualified them to meet the standards of the association. Founded in 1942, the association developed out of a group of physicians who were concerned with the marital problems of their patients. At present the membership is drawn from persons in social work, psychology, medicine, ministry, sociology, education, and law. There are various training centers, accredited or approved by the association which provide preparation for marriage and family counseling. The *AAMFC Register of Health Service Providers in Marital and Family Therapy* is published annually at a cost of $5.00. Copies may be obtained by writing to AAMFC, 225 Yale Avenue, Claremont, California 91711. Included are standards for membership, a code of professional ethics, and other relevant information.

As was indicated above in discussing psychological counselors, there is a wide discrepancy in the training and experience of those who offer their services as marriage counselors through such media as telephone listings and printed leaflets. For this reason, the pastor will wish to assure himself of the qualifications of a marriage counselor prior to referral.

Family Service Association of America.

The Family Service Association of America is a national, accrediting, standard-setting federation for more than 300 nonprofit, voluntary, family social services and marriage counseling agencies throughout North America. Founded in 1911, this organization publishes a *Directory of Member Agencies* which is available for $7.50 through the home office at 44 East 23rd Street, New York, New York, 10010. Clergymen often find the services of the FSA helpful in dealing with certain family problems. The agencies affiliated with FSA offer a variety of services including marriage counseling for husband and wife, parent-child counseling for help in resolving problems between the generations, and assistance in the care of an older parent or member of the family who is mentally ill. Many agencies have homemaker services and offer child care services such as foster home placement and adoption. Information regarding local groups can be obtained through the directory, or by calling the United Givers Fund or Community Chest. A free catalogue of publications about marriage counseling and other social work programs is available through the New York office.

National Association for Retarded Citizens.

The National Association for Retarded Citizens (formerly the National Association for Retarded Children) 2709 Avenue E East, P.O. Box 6109, Arlington, Texas 76011, is a voluntary organization dedicated to the welfare of the mentally retarded of all ages. The national office makes available various publications and bibliographies and provides information on state and local associations. Services of local groups include consultation and evaluation clinics, preschool instruction, summer day camps, and sheltered workshops. Of value to the minister is information regarding individual and group counseling of parents whose child is retarded.

Child Guidance Clinics.

In addition to Family Service Associations and the outpatient counseling facilities of medical schools, many urban communities have one or more groups or agencies devoted specifically to the treatment of children. Although there is no unified title or association for these organizations, it is possible to discover both their availability and qualifications through the local community council or through the Child Welfare League listed previously.

Psychiatric Outpatient Clinics.

In recent years there has developed a program of providing psychiatric treatment through community clinics. Financed by funds from national, state and local governments, these clinics offer a variety of services including intake and evaluation as well as long-term psychotherapy. In addition, there is often follow-up treatment for parolees of State Hospitals including chemical and group therapy. Information regarding such clinics can be obtained from the state public welfare offices or from local Community Chest or UGF councils.

Private Organizations

Although many of the services indicated in the previous section are private in the sense that they do not receive tax funds, there are certain groups which are completely voluntary since they not only receive no tax monies but also do not participate in community chests or UGF drives. The suggested listings included here are indicative of the types of services available to the minister.

Alcoholics Anonymous

Alcoholics Anonymous is a non-profit organization dedicated to the primary purpose of helping alcoholics obtain sobriety. With national offices at P. O. Box 459, Grand Central Station, New York, New York, 10017, AA has local groups or chapters in every city of any size as well as in most smaller towns and communities. In more recent years there has developed a group composed of families of alcoholics known as Al-Anon. Information regarding local groups can be obtained through the classified section of the telephone book or from the New York offices. In addition, the national office makes available a wide variety of publications regarding alcoholism and the treatment of alcoholics.

Planned Parenthood

The Planned Parenthood Federation of America, Inc., maintains offices at 810 Seventh Avenue, New York, New York 10019, Phone: 212-541-7800. In addition there are regional offices as follows:

Western Region: 785 Market Street, Room 1017, San Francisco, California 94103, Phone: 415-777-1217. (Alaska, Arizona, California, Colorado, Hawaii, Idaho, Montana, Nevada, North Dakota, Oregon, South Dakota, Utah, Washington, Wyoming)

South Central Region: Lavaca Square, Suite 201, 302 W. 15th Street, Austin, Texas 78701, Phone: 512-472-4075. (Arkansas, Iowa, Kansas, Louisiana, Missouri, Nebraska, New Mexico, Oklahoma, Texas)

Great Lakes Region: 234 State Street, Suite 802, Detroit, Michigan 48226, Phone: 313-962-4390. (Illinois, Indiana, Michigan, Minnesota, Ohio, West Virginia, Wisconsin)

Southeast Region: 3030 Peachtree Road, N.W., Room 303, Atlanta, Georgia 30305, Phone: 404-262-1128. (Alabama, Florida, Georgia, Kentucky, Mississippi, North Carolina, South Carolina, Tennessee, Virginia)

North Atlantic Region: 810 Seventh Avenue, New York, New York 10019, Phone: 212-541-7800. (Connecticut, Delaware, District of Columbia, Maine, Maryland, Massachusetts, New Hampshire, New Jersey, New York, Pennsylvania, Rhode Island, Vermont)

Primarily concerned with information and research, this organization makes available a list of affiliates and publications about planned parenthood. In many urban areas there are consultants who will meet with responsible individuals and groups for the purpose of exploring the implications of parenthood and world population.

Red Cross

The International Red Cross is best known for its service in time of emergency or disaster. In addition, many chapters provide referral resources for situations involving servicemen and women. Information is available through listings in local telephone directories.

YMCA & YWCA

There are branches of both YMCA and YWCA in most urban communities. Although in the strictest sense of the word these groups do not provide generalized referral services, certain local branches often have programs of rehabilitation for young people as well as adults. Since these services vary quite widely from city to city, the best course of action would be for the pastor to consult with the branch in his own community to discover the kinds of resources available.

Religious Groups

Through the years religious groups have provided a variety of services to those in need. While it is obviously impossible to list all such services here, the ones included indicate the types of resources available to the minister for referral.

Catholic Charities

The Catholic Church supports some 400 diocesan agencies and branch offices and, in addition, is affiliated with over 600 institutions of charity including maternity homes, settlements, day care centers, homes for the aged, institutions for neglected or delinquent children, and the like. In many communities family and child guidance services are available. A complete listing of these agencies and institutions for the United States, Puerto Rico, and Canada may be obtained for $3.50 plus postage from the National Conference of Catholic Charities, 1346 Connecticut Avenue, N. W., Washington, D. C., 20036.

Jewish Health and Welfare Agencies

Services provided through the Jewish Health and Welfare agencies include family counseling, day nurseries, convalescent homes, sheltered workshops, vocational and rehabilitational counseling, etc. A complete listing of these services can be purchased for $3.00 from the Council of Jewish Federations, 575 Lexington Avenue, New York, New York, 10022. In addition to listing its own affiliates, this publication provides a most helpful appendix describing other directories and service available in various areas of the United States and Canada.

Rescue Missions

Most urban areas have one or more rescue missions. Ordinarily, the services performed include room and lodging for destitute individuals, together with personal counseling, job placement, and religious nurture. As might be expected, such groups vary widely in emphasis and effectiveness. Information can be obtained from listings in the telephone book or from local councils of churches.

The Salvation Army

From its inception, the Salvation Army has rendered a wide variety of services to persons in need. These include hospitals, children's homes, foster care, settlements and day nurseries, men's social service centers, boys' clubs, missing person's bureaus, employment service, and the like. In addition, the Salvation Army maintains ten maternity homes and hospitals and ten maternity homes. Information concerning these homes and hospitals can be obtained from the following regional offices:

Eastern Territory, 120 West 14th Street, New York, New York 10011, two maternity homes and hospitals, two maternity homes.

Central Territory, 860 North Dearborn Street, Chicago, Illinois, 60610, five maternity homes and hospitals, one maternity home.

Southern Territory, 1424 Northeast Expressway, Atlanta, Georgia, 30329, two maternity homes and hospitals.

Western Territory, 30840 Hawthorne Boulevard, Rancho Palos

Verdes, California 90274, one maternity home and hospital, seven maternity homes.

The national office is located at 120 West 14th Street, New York, New York. In addition to information regarding maternity homes and hospitals, the regional territories listed above also provide information concerning the various activities of the Salvation Army.

Summary

Although not exhaustive, the listing of referral resources included here indicates the type of service available to the minister as he seeks to help his parishioners in time of need. Some of these groups have been in existence for many years, whereas others are of comparatively recent origin. In every case the organization came into being as a consequence of one or more persons becoming aware of some pressing need which was not being adequately met. Despite the fact that the resources available today far outreach those of only a few decades ago, there is still much suffering to be relieved. Thus, it is possible that someone who reads these words may set in motion the forces required to render a service to still other groups of persons who presently must struggle alone in their search for wholeness.

CHAPTER—5
Special Problems in Referral

Throughout the discussion it has been apparent that the matter of referral is by definition beset with pitfalls and obstacles. While there are many instances in which all that is needed is information regarding the proper source for help, it is not very likely that the providing of such information will be the end of the matter. The very fact that the person is in need of help is indicative of the possibility that the course ahead will not be completely smooth. And in the instances where referral involves much more than simple impartation of knowledge, there are sure to be many tangled strands which will be the occasion for distress and heartache before the situation is resolved.

Although space will not allow a consideration of the varieties of such problems, the principles involved can be inferred by looking in some detail at a few. In the sections which follow we will examine the issues posed by the restrictions of privileged communication, the situation in which referral is resisted by members of the family of the parishioner, and the continuing possibilities open when referral seems to fail.

Privileged Communication

In most instances, referral requires some kind of communication between the person doing the referring and the person to whom the referral is made; and by definition, such communication always occurs when there is consultation regarding the situation of another person. The problem emerges at the point of the referring person's responsibility toward his patient or parishioner, as the case may be, with regard to information which may have been given to him in confidence but which seems important if the referral is to succeed. The question turns on how much freedom, either from a moral or a legal point of view, can be assumed or exercised by the person doing the referring.

It is likely that many ministers have never bothered to raise the question of professional communication, privileged or otherwise. Yet, as others can testify from painful experience, it is a matter which is fraught with danger—including the possibility of legal action for libel or slander. Such action is particularly prevalent among those whose very difficulties tend to distort their own sense of values and who find themselves striking out in ways which would ordinarily be quite foreign to their ordinary manner of life.

Usually, the question of privileged communication is discussed in terms of whether the minister or physician or whoever was helping a person or persons in distress can be compelled by a court of law to reveal information which was received in confidence. The laws vary from state to state on this issue,[1] and my impression is that most ministers have little if any understanding of their status under the law. Through the years, as this question has been raised in seminars and workshops, it has been increasingly clear to me that ministers tend to use their own judgment—whatever the law may be. Thus, if they felt it would be detrimental to a parishioner to reveal something told in confidence, they would be willing to be cited for contempt of court before breaking the confidence; at the same time, if they felt that the revealing of confidential information would be of benefit to the parishioner, they would be willing to run the risk of breach of confidence—whatever the consequence to themselves.

When privileged communication is considered not from the standpoint of whether the person can be required to reveal a confidence but from the standpoint of his freedom to reveal the confidence without the permission of the patient or parishioner, the matter relates much more directly to the question of referral. Ordinarily it is

[1] The most thorough study of this question to my knowledge is *The Right To Silence*, by William Harold Tiemann, John Knox Press, Richmond, Virginia, 1964.

assumed that a profession or group which enjoys privileged communication, i.e. cannot be required by law to reveal information received in confidence, also works under much more rigid restrictions against voluntary revealing of such information. By the same token, a profession or group which does not enjoy privileged communication has more latitude in revealing confidential information. The theory behind such an assumption is logical enough. Presumably, the person giving the information to a member of a non-privileged group would know full well that it might be revealed, whereas the same person consulting a member of a privileged group would expect that the information would go no further. In actual practice, however, it is likely that the patients or parishioners have even less awareness of the law than do physicians or ministers, and it seems safe to assume that their expectation is that their confidences will be kept inviolate no matter what the law.

There is, of course, an obviously simple solution to the whole matter, and that is to obtain the permission of the patient or parishioner to confer or consult with another professional person. In some cases such permission must be in writing, although generally speaking clear and unambiguous oral consent may be sufficient. From a moral point of view, the minister would certainly be most desirous of working completely in the open as far as his parishioner was concerned. Moreover, as we have seen in various illustrations already cited, a significant aspect of the referral is the parishioner's awareness that he and the minister are working together toward the goal of his own welfare and that they cooperate at every point to attain this goal. Thus, a healing as well as a moral purpose is served by this kind of frank and mutual participation in the referral or consultation. While it would usually be unnecessary, if not ridiculous, for the minister to require that the parishioner sign a statement authorizing him to consult with another professional person, the notion of consent is of inestimable value.

The fact is, however, that there are times when such consent cannot be responsibly given. If the person is not in contact with reality or if it appears that the mere suggestion of consultation or referral will prevent any further opportunity for help, then the minister is forced to reach a decision on his own. Recognizing the variations in legal statutes, the general rule of thumb is that if the information given is accurate and if the intention behind its being given is clearly and unambiguously to help the person, then there is sufficient justification to reveal what was given in confidence.

Such a judgment is, by definition, subjective and thus open to all manner of distortions. Inevitably opinion colors fact, and intention is notoriously difficult to assess. Yet, it is precisely the willingness to make decisions in the absence of any hard and fast rule that is the mark of the professional person—he weighs all aspects and then is willing to assume the risk involved in helping his patient or parishioner. Such an assumption can never be taken lightly. Any and all information is treated with the same enormous respect as that accorded of the person, himself. But when the well-being of the person is at stake, then all else is of secondary consideration.

Family Resistance to Referral

One of the problems encountered in referral is the possibility of resistance on the part of the family of the person referred. For all manner of reasons, the persons nearest to the parishioner experiencing difficulty may find themselves threatened by the fact that their son or daughter, husband or wife, brother or sister is in need of help which thus far they have been unable to provide. There is still enough social stigma attached to the need for psychiatric help to make this kind of therapy unacceptable to many otherwise enlightened persons. So it is that the suggestion to consult a psychiatrist inevitably meets with a denial on the part of such persons.

This was the situation involving the student whose circumstance was set forth in the first chapter. After consulting the Dean of the college, the minister called a psychiatrist who agreed to see the student the same afternoon. After a brief interview, the psychiatrist insisted that hospitalization was essential on the grounds that the student was suffering from severe paranoid delusions. Accordingly, the student was admitted to the psychiatric section of a local hospital where he was placed under intensive care. When the pastor called on him later in the day, he complained that the hospital furniture was wired and that it was impossible for him to sit in a chair, to lie in a bed, or to be near a table for fear of being electrocuted. Thus, he found it necessary to pace up and down in order to avoid the magnetic waves which were being directed at him.

Meanwhile, the college authorities had contacted the student's family by phone, advising them of his condition and indicating the course of action that had been followed. In less than twelve hours, the student's father and older brother arrived and berated the college officials for taking the student to a psychiatrist and agreeing to his being hospitalized. After a lengthy conference with the psychiatrist, they withdrew the student from the hospital against orders, gathered all his belongings together, and took him home. Although they were unable to see the minister who had suggested consulting the psychiatrist, they told the Dean that their initial thought was to sue him for libel but that they had changed their minds.

Subsequently, it was learned that the student had already been a patient in the State Hospital near his home whence he had been removed against the doctor's orders. On that occasion, as in the present situation, the family had said that he was "simply nervous," and all he needed was to "take it easy in his own home." It is, of course, not possible to indicate what might have been the outcome had he been able to receive professional help. The actual outcome is known, however. After a period of several weeks at home, he was committed to the State Hospital where, according to last reports, he is still a patient with a very poor prognosis.

A similar situation is reported by a minister whose account of his concern for his parishioner includes the frustration of knowing that his efforts were resented by her family. The parishioner, Lucille, was in her late teens, exceptionally able in her studies at school, and scholastically ahead of her own age group, having taken extra work in summer sessions. Active in the work of the Church, she had often talked with the pastor about her home life where she felt "trapped" by reason of her parents' lack of understanding. In the weeks immediately prior to the interview reported here, she indicated that she had been vaguely "afraid of something," and that on one occasion she had been sure someone had broken into their house at night even though a later investigation revealed no evidence of such an entry.

The pastor requested permission from her to confer with the family physician, and together it seemed to them that she should be seen by a psychiatrist. Although there was some resistance on the part of her father, Lucille was admitted to a hospital in a nearby city for complete tests and diagnosis. No physical disability appeared, but during her hospitalization she became greatly disturbed. On one occasion, when the pastor called, she confided that she wanted to see the psychiatrist regularly, but that her family had vetoed the proposal. She indicated that she did not want to return home, since she feared that "she would get worse."

Following this visit, the minister called on the parents and indicated his hope that she could receive psychotherapy as soon as possible. The father strongly opposed such treatment, insisting that she was simply "tired out" from being "on the go" so much and that all she needed was to be let alone since "people paid too much attention to her." In spite of his resistance, Lucille did continue in the hospital for several weeks, during which time she was seen with some regularity by the psychiatrist.

Shortly after Lucille's return home, the minister visited her. After initial greetings, she had little to say. The conversation with the family was somewhat strained, and after a short while, he left.

The next week Lucille called the church for an appointment. She sounded depressed. At the scheduled time the following interview took place.

1. *Minister:* Hi. Come in. It's good to see you.

2. *Lucille:* Hi. I hear you need someone to help with the mimeograph while the secretary is sick.

3. *Minister:* Well, it sure would be nice. We couldn't pay you what you are worth, but maybe you'd get a star or two in your crown!

4. *Lucille:* Whatever you'd pay me would be more than I'm worth. I've just got to talk to you. I'm getting so depressed again. The thing that's really bothering me is . . .

(At this moment the outer door of the church opened, and her father appeared, coming quickly to the study.)

5. *Minister:* Well, come in. Glad to see you. (Father came in, took a chair, and said nothing.)

6. *Minister:* Glad to see you. It's been several days.

7. *Father:* Yeah . . .

8. *Minister:* What's on your mind? You look like you're in a hurry.

9. *Father:* Oh, I just came over to get in on all the secrets! I like to keep up on all the secrets!

10. *Minister:* Guess you came to the wrong place, then. I'm the last to hear any secrets around here.

11. *Father:* Well, I just want to get in on all the secrets, that's all.

12. *Minister:* All right. If I hear of any and can share them, I'll tell you. (long silence, quite heavy and painful)

13. *Lucille:* Mr. M., I have to write a theme on the land of Canaan. Do you have any material I could use?

14. *Minister:* Yes, but right now the books are at home. You could stop by there and get them, or I can bring them over tomorrow. Also the library has several good atlases.

15. *Lucille:* O.K. I'll try the library. And if you'll bring the books tomorrow I'll stop by and get them.

(Another long silence. Felt quite uncomfortable, particularly with what this was doing to Lucille. Began to talk of some projects around the church, drawing her father into the conversation as much as possible. There was another rather long silence.)

16. *Father:* Well, Lucille, it's about time for us to go.

17. *Lucille:* I think I'll stay around for a little while.

18. *Father:* Now, look. If you have anything to say to Mr. M., why just go ahead and say it. I don't think there is anything a family can't discuss together in front of the pastor. There's no reason for secrets in a family. If you have anything to say, just say it right out, with me here. (He spoke rapidly, and a little heated.)

19. *Lucille:* But, Dad, I just came by to talk to Mr. M. about a book.

20. *Father:* Well, he said he doesn't have it. I guess we can go on home now. Are you ready?

21. *Lucille:* I don't want to go home just now. I want to stay around here for a little while.

22. *Father:* Well, there's no reason to stay around here any longer.

If you want to talk to Mr. M., just go ahead and talk. We don't need any secrets in our family.

23. *Lucille:* Dad, I told you I came to ask about a book.

24. *Father:* He doesn't have it. Let's go. (Father stood up. Lucille stood up more slowly, looking at her hands, which she had clasped in front of her.)

25. *Lucille:* Well, Mr. M., thanks, anyhow. I'll try to get by tomorrow for the book.

26. *Minister:* I'm sorry I can't be of any help. I guess you came at the wrong time. Most of my books are at home right now.

27. *Lucille:* Well, thanks anyway. I'll see you tomorrow if I can.

28. *Minister:* I'll be looking for you. You two take good care, now.

29. *Father:* See you Sunday.

In commenting on the interview, the minister confessed that he did not know what to do, that he felt throughout a strong sympathy for the young girl but at every point found himself blocked by the resistance of her father. Neither then nor later did he find it possible to deal openly with the father in terms of his negative feelings. To use his words, "I felt helpless and inexperienced." He recognized that both Lucille and her father needed help but saw himself prevented from being a pastor to either.

There are several significant aspects of referral which appear in these two illustrations. In the first place, there is a realistic limit beyond which the minister cannot go in encouraging his parishioners to avail themselves of the help that is needed and that is at hand. In certain instances, ministers have found themselves involved in awkward situations because of their assuming a responsibility which went beyond their rightful place. To put the matter quite plainly, the minister does not have the authority to institute commitment proceedings. However much he may believe a person is in need of hospitalization, it is not his prerogative to attempt to set in motion the procedures which are prescribed by the state laws for this purpose. This does not mean that he cannot indicate to the family his concern for the parishioner and his judgment that together they should seek some competent person to assist them in arriving at a decision. Indeed, one of his primary functions may be to enable the family to come to grips with their own resistances against psychotherapy or hospitalization. But this is quite different from his assuming the responsibility which is not his either legally or morally.

In the second place, there is the necessity for the pastor to assess his true role in being of help to the parishioner who is obviously in trouble. In each of these two illustrations, the relationship between the minister and the directly involved parishioner was good; but in both cases the minister's relationship to the family of the parishioner was quite poor. In such a situation it soon becomes evident that the most direct access to the parishioner may lie through being of help to the affected members of the family. As many ministers can testify, this is a lesson that is difficult to learn. Almost inevitably, there tends to be a feeling of resentment or hostility toward those whose behavior seems so inimical to the person of immediate concern. Thus, it is exceedingly difficult to see the family as persons who also have needs; whose behavior attests to their own distress; and who may, in the end, be the key to the distress of the person immediately involved.

Of course, in certain instances, it is not possible to be of help to the family for a variety of reasons. In the situation of the college student, for example, it is not likely that the local minister had any real opportunity to relate to the father and brother in any meaningful way. Their presence in town allowed time only for gathering together the student's belongings and packing him up for the trip home. Such was not the case in the second illustration, however. Here the impediment lay not in the circumstance of the family but in the insecurity of the minister. In retrospect, there is no way to predict what might have been the outcome had the minister been able to relate to the father directly at the point of his resistance to his daughter's receiving help. It is, of course, quite possible that they would have ended in the same place. At the same time, it is also possible that the father might have found the help he needed to deal with his own fears and anxieties and as a consequence might have been able to stand with his daughter in her distress rather than continue to deny that she was having any problem at all. In line with the principles we have been considering, here seems to be a place where referral is strongly indicated, since evidently the pastor finds the situation more than he can handle on his own resources.

Finally, the pastor's assessment of his own role in such a circumstance will include a realistic appraisal of whether his relationship with the directly involved parishioner is primarily motivated for the good of the parishioner or for his own good. It is, of course, inevitable that he be concerned for himself in the relationship, and nothing here is intended to suggest that this kind of self-concern can be nonexistent or is necessarily negative. The clue, however, is whether it is primary or secondary.

It is not possible to say with any certainty just how this factor was operative in the two illustrations. In the second case, the pastor may have found himself taking sides with the daughter against the father to such an extent that he could not really be of any help to the daughter. Put in other words, the daughter might have become a tool by which the pastor was able to fight the father in retaliation for his negative attitude. In that event, his judgment about what was best for the daughter would almost certainly be impaired. Conceivably, he could wish that she would have to go to the hospital simply as a means of bringing more pain to the father. Although such a possibility may be rather far-fetched in this instance, it is certain that the minister ignores it to the peril of the parishioner. The very movement of the interview suggests quite strongly that far more was taking place than meets the eye. And there are few persons, ministers included, who can find themselves caught in the middle of a family disagreement without tending to take sides and thus lose their perspective.

In the first illustration, it is even more tenuous to trace this kind of possibility. No actual conversation took place between the minister and the student's father and brother. Yet the fact that the minister took the pains to discover that the student had been hospitalized before and subsequently reported that he was again in the hospital with a negative prognosis might give rise to the speculation that he had something of an "I told you so" feeling toward the father and the brother. If this were the case, then he might have found himslf desiring the hospitalization of the student simply to vindicate his own position and to demonstrate the error of the family.

When Referral Fails

It is inevitable that in certain instances the referral will not succeed. There is no way to predict in advance that the parishioner will be able to respond to the therapist or that the kind of help offered will be sufficient to effect a resolution of the difficulty. At such times the importance of the relationship between the pastor and the parishioner at the time of referral cannot be overestimated. If the referral has been effected in such a way that the pastor seems convinced that the person to whom the parishioner is referred will certainly be able to help, then the possibility of renewing his relationship to the parishioner in the light of the failure becomes much more difficult. In the same vein, if the referral has been effected in such a way that the pastor is no longer involved in the life of the parishioner, the renewal of the relationship is sure to be hard. On the other hand, if it has been clear throughout that the pastor is truly concerned for the welfare of the parishioner, honestly believes that other help is needed and that this or that person can provide the help, but frankly states that there is no way to guarantee that help will inevitably come, he is then in a position to stand with the parishioner in a continued search for help from other sources.

Although somewhat of an oversimplification, it is possible to recognize two general categories in regard to persons for whom a referral has not been successful—for whatever reason. The first, and by all odds the most frustrating for the pastor, is the situation wherein the person does not really recognize or acknowledge a need for help. The other, obviously, is the situation of the person who genuinely wants help, but apparently does not improve in the referral experience.

Illustrative of the first of these is the previously discussed experience of the student with the man outside the chapel. In commenting on the situation, the student noted that the man did see the pastor, who then persuaded him to consult a psychiatrist. No account is given of the process whereby the pastor accomplished this purpose, but the man did go. Subsequently he reported that he was glad he went, since, in his words, "I really believe I did him some good!" It was at this point that the pastor reported his complete frustration in that he simply did not have any idea what to do.

Similar illustrations could be multiplied by every parish minister. The mother who comes asking that the minister get her son to see the school counselor, the wife who comes imploring the minister to get her husband to AA, the daughter who comes urging that the minister persuade her parents to seek help in their marriage—these and countless others represent the need and the frustration of unwilling referral. In such situations, the minister finds his position precarious on two fronts. If he is unsuccessful in getting the distressed person to seek professional help, he runs the risk of alienating the one who has brought the problem to him. At the same time, if he persuades the distressed person to seek help against his will, he runs the risk of jeopardizing the possibility of his being of help when, finally, it is desired. It would be comforting to say that if the minister would follow certain simple rules of procedure, he would always be successful in avoiding this double jeopardy. Obviously, such is not the case. Nevertheless, there are certain general principles which provide guidelines.

In the first place, the minister's relationship to the person who has asked help for another must always be quite open and unambiguous. As we have already noted, the one who comes is "the bird in the hand," and in many instances this person is the only access the minister may have to the individual in obvious distress. If, without disregarding the problems of the third person, the minister can concentrate on the person at hand, he may be able to take some of the burden on himself and thus enable this person to be more helpful to the one in trouble. As everyone knows, there is a terrible strain in living with an alcoholic, or a young person whose life is twisted and distorted, or a couple whose marriage is falling apart. Members of the family who live under such conditions become hurt themselves and often quite inadvertently tend to punish the offending persons when their overt purpose is to be of help. When the minister is able to assist in their working through their own feelings with regard to the third person, there is a genuine possibility that they may in fact become more able to help than they were before. The temptation for the minister is to concentrate on the third person entirely and thus overlook the pastoral opportunity with the person who is present. More subtly, he may find that he is uncomfortable in his relationship to the person who has come and thus rationalizes that his energies should certainly be devoted to the person who is much more obviously in distress. In sum, the minister's first responsibility is to the person at hand—not in the sense of facile agreement to intervene in the life of the third person, but in the sense of genuine pastoral care here and now.

The second principle follows from the first. Just as the minister's relationship to the parishioner who comes must be clearly focused on that person and his needs, so his relationship to the third person must be clearly and unambiguously based on a concern for him. This is to say that he can never come as an emissary who must report back to someone else. The minute he falls into such a trap, the third person becomes an object to be manipulated rather than a person to be helped. Moreover, in such a situation, the minister inevitably feels that his ability is at stake, that he must produce results or else be found wanting. This does not mean that he must avoid all reference to his previous conversation when he goes to the third person. It does mean that while he will most certainly be concerned for the interests of the person who came, his primary concern when he actually calls on the third person is that person. In a word, he goes because he genuinely wants to help him, not because his going will make somebody else feel better.

In the light of these principles, the minister is able to approach the unwilling parishioner with much more freedom and, thus, with much more possibility of success. The following brief excerpt illustrates the process which is similar in many ways to the situation described in the fabricated verbatim toward the end of the section entitled "When Referral Is Resisted" in Chapter Three.

1. *Minister:* Joe, I appreciate your coming by, and imagine that you didn't much want to. I know things haven't been going so well at

school; and I thought if we talked about it, we might find some way out.

2. *Joe:* Aw, there's nothing to say. Did Mother tell you to talk to me?

3. *Minister:* She and I have talked about the situation, and she did ask me to see you. That's not the main reason for my doing it, however. After I heard about the trouble, I'd have tried to see you even if she hadn't suggested it. I really was sorry to learn that things have been so tough, and I'd like to help if I could.

4. *Joe:* Well, she's been ganging everybody up on me, so I imagined she'd put you up to this.

5. *Minister:* Like I say, that's not why I'm here; but I guess it's hard for you to see it any other way. Sort of feel like I'm ganged up against you, too.

6. *Joe:* Yeah. Gee, Reverend, why don't they just get off my back? If they'd just let me alone, it'd be all right.

7. *Minister:* I guess I can't speak for anybody but myself, and I surely don't want to be on your back. If I can't help then I'll get out. I guess you're saying you got enough folks riding you now without taking on any more.

8. *Joe:* Gosh, yeah! It's just nag, nag, nag all the time. I've just got sick and tired of it.

Thus far in the interview the minister has attempted to state his concern for the student and, at the same time, to recognize the resistance that stands between them like a barrier. He has not fallen into the trap of attempting to coerce the student into seeing the school counselor "for his own good," nor has he been drawn into a defensive argument with regard to his conversation with the student's mother. He frankly wants Joe to undertake whatever steps are necessary to work out the distress, but he is willing to move at a pace more nearly matching the resistance than an exhortation would. He knows that seeing the school counselor has much to commend it, but he also knows that in Joe's present circumstance, he may be unable to accept the help that is offered. His long-range hope, therefore, is that his relationship to Joe will be such that if the visit to the school counselor is not successful, they will be able to work toward some other resource which may prove to be the means for resolution. Later in the interview the following excerpt occurred.

53. *Minister:* I honestly would like for you to see the school counselor. At least we'd be no worse off, and she may be able to help more than now seems apparent.

54. *Joe:* Gosh, I don't know. There's some real kooks go up there to see her, and I'd hate to be like them.

55. *Minister:* Yeah, I see what you mean. People might begin to think you were nuts or something if you went.

56. *Joe:* That's right. (pause) You don't think I'm nuts, do you?

57. *Minister:* Heavens no! But I do think you've gotten crossways with a lot of things and that you're having a rough time because of it. What I'd like to see is that you get these things straightened out so you could start feeling better again and not always be butting your head against a stone wall. I think she can help, and that's why I'd like for you to see her. Of course, I may be wrong. She might not help. In that case, I'd like for us to look somewhere else. I know there's an answer somewhere, and I want us to find it.

58. *Joe:* Well, I don't know. I guess it'd be O.K. to go up there one time. You really believe she's all right?

59. *Minister:* I know her pretty well, and I'm sure she's good. What I don't know is whether she'll be able to help you. That's something no one could know beforehand. I hope she can.

60. *Joe:* All right. I'll let you know how it comes out.

It seems likely that this student was actually eager for help, but had not found any way to accept it. His final statement indicates that he has come to feel that he and the minister are on the same side, and it is quite probable that he can now return with either a positive or a negative report on his visit to the school counselor. In that event, the minister will be able to rejoice with him if the report is good, or help him look elsewhere if it is bad.

It goes without saying that not every such interview is marked by this kind of success. The person may be so defensive, so threatened, so hostile that there is little possibility for the establishing of such a relationship as is evident here. Even so, the principles are the same, whatever the outcome.

We have been discussing the situation in which the parishioner does not recognize a need for help—or resists acknowledging this need. The other general category includes those persons who genuinely want to be helped, but apparently do not find it in the referral experience. As can be inferred from the brief excerpt just cited, when the relationship with the pastor is that of a mutual seeking for help, it is possible for the parishioner to return with a negative report without being put in the position of inferring that the pastor was wrong in the referral. Since from the outset the pastor has not in any sense suggested that the referral is bound to succeed, he leaves the way open to continue his help in spite of the fact that the first attempt did not work out. While such a relationship is clearly desirable, there are certain subtle dangers which should not be overlooked.

In the first place, the minister may jeopardize the referral experience by indicating the possibility of its failure. In a sincere and genuine attempt to avoid any intimation that sure success will certainly accompany the referral, he may subtly prejudice the case in a negative fashion. There is a thin line between these two, and every minister can attest that it is difficult to walk. The dangers of falling off on either side can easily be described. Avoiding the dangers, however, is not so easily done.

Alongside this tension, there is an even more subtle danger. It is possible that the minister does not really want the parishioner to find help from the referral experience and, thus, does not really let him go. Somewhere within him, he may be threatened by the fact that he cannot be the means for help to all persons under all circumstances. Thus, while overtly he seems to be sending the parishioner to another helper, he tends to make sure that the referral will fail; thus the parishioner will have to return to him as the true and final source of help after all. There are no readily recognizable indices to which one may point as evidence of this attitude. Nevertheless, it is one to which many ministers fall victim, and every pastor needs to examine himself from time to time simply to make a realistic assessment of his own dealings with his parishioners with regard to their being helped by someone other than himself.

Finally, the necessary provision for a continued relationship with the parishioner who wants help and who does not find it in the first referral experience must be guarded lest the parishioner make the seeking for help a substitute for accepting help. As we have already seen, there is a subtle yet powerful resistance to help even in those who overtly seek it. The secondary gains of trouble, such as receiving attention, having an excuse for failure, or being relieved of obligations, can never be overlooked. Thus, the parishioner may go from person to person, always apparently asking for help, but making sure that it never comes. When this situation appears, the responsibility of the pastor focuses not on assisting the parishioner to find still another source for help but rather working through what it means that help can never actually be accepted.

Conclusion

Although these are by no means the only problems encountered in a ministry of referral, it is possible to see by implication the kinds of principles which are relevant to a wide variety of difficulties. Inevitably, the course is not easy. By definition, the person who is suffering distress is unable to function in a normal fashion. Added to this are the minister's own feelings, not always resolved, regarding his admission of inadequacy and his necessity for taking a secondary role in the restoration of his parishioner. Under such circumstances, it is surprising that referral often goes as smoothly as it does.

The root of the matter, always, is the pastor's genuine concern to see the parishioner helped, regardless of the source from which the help comes. When this concern exists, the principles discussed here will be of value; without this concern, very little of a constructive nature can be done.

CHAPTER—6
The On-Going Ministry

Thus far our discussion has been primarily concerned with the relationship of the pastor to the parishioner, at the time of crisis when it appeared that some additional help would be needed if the presenting problem was to be resolved. Inevitably, such a discussion implies a much wider range of relationships which are also involved in the restoration of the person in distress. In this concluding chapter, we shall look briefly at three aspects of these wider relationships which must be taken into account if the referral experience is to be successful. These are the supporting role of the community during the referral experience, the relationship to the parishioner following the referral experience, and the underlying factors in a continuing ministry which builds upon the healing experience of the crisis situation.

Supporting Role of the Community

By definition the ministry of referral is intensely personal. For the time being the pastor concentrates on the situation being encountered by the parishioner in the hope that sufficient resources can be found to effect his recovery. The parishioner and his family, at times, seem to be temporarily isolated from the community, as their accustomed relationships are disrupted and they find themselves forced to search for untried paths. It is a painful way, made more so because there is no assurance that the path chosen will lead to the desired goal. Into this intense experience the pastor comes to stand with them and to enable them to deal with whatever the experience may bring.

The fact is, however, that the isolation is illusory. No matter how disrupted the accustomed relationships, the persons experiencing the distress are still a part of a community. And the community, by its relationship to them in such a time can often spell the difference between success and failure. It is this enormous potential for good or evil, for creativity or destruction that can never be overlooked by the pastor if his ministry of reconciliation and resolution is to be of benefit to those who come suddenly or gradually to a crisis.

It is a truism that troubles come in two varieties. On the one hand, there are the troubles which are socially acceptable—those which have no stigma attached. On the occasion of such trouble the community rallies around and gives its support to the person in distress. For example, there is a death in the family—neighbors and friends immediately come by to share the sad burden of bereavement. Or a home burns down—offers pour in to provide clothing, a place to stay, and help in patching up the disrupted fabric of life. An operation is needed—there are those who help with baby-sitting and the providing of meals while the wife and mother is in the hospital. The list could go on and on, but the point is readily apparent. The hurt and grief is no less intense because the distress is socially acceptable; but the presence of the community is a powerful factor in helping bridge the gap caused by the disruption in normal life.

On the other hand, there are troubles which are not socially acceptable—those to which there is a stigma attached. On the occasion of these troubles, the community seems uncertain in its relationship to the persons in distress. It may censure or scorn; it may wish to help, but find no ready approach; it may pass by on the other side simply because it does not know what to do or how to do it. Such troubles are legion. There is the teen-age girl who finds herself pregnant out of wedlock; there is the affair with a secretary which threatens to destroy a marriage; there is the uncontrolled use of alcohol which casts a blight over the entire family; there is the emotional disturbance which renders the person incapable of dealing rationally with life. In these and a host of others the apparent isolation stands out with awesome threat. There is no overt rallying of the community, there is no easy access to the damaged relationships.

To describe these two types of troubles is not to deal with the rightness or wrongness of community attitude, is not to condone stigma or blame, and is not to defend a dual system. It is simply a recognition of that which *is*, as every pastor can attest. Nor is such a description to imply that there are no exceptions. Here, again, every pastor can point with satisfaction to those occasions wherein members of his congregation did in fact stand with their fellows who were literally passing through the valley of the shadow of death, and by this community of suffering and of healing enabled them to come out on the other side. Happily such exceptions do exist. Unhappily, they are all too often just that—exceptions.

Yet it is precisely in the context of these kinds of troubles that the pastor's referral ministry most often lies. It is easy to see why. When the acceptable troubles befall a person, there appears to be no particular problem calling on whatever resources are available in the community. On occasion there may be lack of knowledge as to the availability of such resources, but this lack is not difficult to fill. Yet when the unacceptable troubles come there is more at stake than a simple calling on obvious resources. The very necessity for seeking help is in itself a stumbling block. There is a difficulty in acknowledging the problem, in recognizing the need for help. What happens is that finally the pain and burden become so great that something simply has to be done. But the resistance is not diminished; rather it is matched by another force which is more powerful. In such a circumstance the person turns to another for help, both wanting it and fearing it, hoping against hope that some facile solution can be provided, knowing deep within that the suffering will get worse before it gets better.

These are the complex feelings which make the isolation seem so real. Thus is the seeking of help postponed; thus is the accepting of help fraught with danger. Thus is the pastor's referral ministry rendered more difficult. Thus is the possible recovery of the person made more tenuous.

In the light of these circumstances, it is evident that the pastor's referral ministry actually begins long before the person encounters the crisis and calls for help. Through a constructive program of nurture, the congregation is enabled to understand the nature of human distress and the underlying factors in personal disturbance which all too often do not meet the eye. Discussions on teen-age problems, on alcoholism, on marital tensions, on mental illness help to dispel the misapprehension and misunderstanding which all too often have beset these conditions. It is, of course, too great an oversimplification to suggest that the distinction between acceptable and unacceptable troubles could or will disappear. It is possible, however, to recognize the fact that persons experiencing trouble of whatever sort can be seen in terms of their being helped rather than simply in terms of their being categorized. Under such circumstances, the question becomes not so much concerned with fixing blame or assessing penalty as it does on discovering the avenues for reconciliation and restitution.

As a consequence of this kind of nurture, two things are possible. The most obvious is that the person in distress is more able to seek for and accept help than would otherwise be the case. When the feeling of isolation is diminished by an awareness that the community will understand although it does not condone, the pain of the unacceptable trouble is lessened to the extent that it can be borne as a necessary aspect of its resolution. The resistance does not disappear, but it is more easily overcome. Thus, the minister has a far greater opportunity to help the parishioner face the realistic factors in the situation and set about the proper course for their resolution.

In the second place, such nurture actually tends to diminish the frequency of deep crisis situations where help is sought only as a matter of extreme necessity. While it is true that such violent times often seem needed for the person to come to grips with his situation, it is also true that the danger of destruction is much more real. Every pastor is familiar with the AA rule of thumb that the alcoholic must "hit bottom" before he will honestly take steps to accept the help available. At the same time, such an extremity may come too late for real restitution to be possible. It is this fact that has led to a serious attempt on the part of those who wish to help alcoholics to "raise the bottom," a phrase which has been used to describe the enabling of the parishioner to accept help before everything was lost. The same principle applies to unacceptable difficulties of whatever nature.

When the person perceives that help is available and that there is community support, then the possibility of early resolution is increased many fold.

When the Person Returns

Closely related to the minister's concern that the Church understand and support the person facing distress are the issues posed in the renewal of relationships when the person "comes back" to the community. The return is not always geographical, although it may be—as in the instance when the person has been a patient in a State Hospital or some other institution or clinic away from home. Whether or not the return is spatial, it is always psychological. The sense of isolation which inevitably accompanies severe personal distress may be overcome only gradually. As we saw in the previous section, this bridging of the gap is always a two-way proposition. The return home and the coming out to meet the one returning comprise the two aspects of the reconciliation.

As every pastor knows, there are special problems which confront the person who is making his way back into the mainstream of life. One way to describe the difficulty is to use the metaphor from physics that a vacuum tends to be filled. When a person drops out of his ordinary activities in the home, the community, the business world, there is a vacuum created which is sustained for a short time. Yet, gradually the space which he occupied becomes filled in varieties of ways. The golf foursome fills in for a while and then finds a congenial fourth who begins to play more and more regularly. The person's work at the office is divided and distributed until it becomes a part of the routine of many others. Family plans involving day to day decisions must be made apart from the accustomed desires and opinions of the now absent member. So it is that when the person comes back, he may quite literally discover that there is no real place for him or that the place is greatly reduced in size so that he cannot move freely as was once his custom.

Another way to describe the problem is to see it from the perspective of the community itself. Although to speak of the community as though it were a unified whole presents a false picture, since it is made up of varying individuals, there is nonetheless a sense in which there tends to be a common reaction. By and large, people do not really know what to do with a person who comes back, particularly if the nature of his absence involves some sort of nonacceptable trouble. They are not sure what to expect of him, whether they should attempt to pick up where they left off, whether they should approach him somewhat tentatively, whether they should make reference to the trouble or ignore it. In the presence of this kind of uncertainty, many people tend to avoid the problem by simply avoiding the person.

Still another way to understand the complexity of the return is to explore the mingled feelings of the person himself. Healing is always a process, sometimes slower than others. At some point or other the time comes when the person is apparently well enough to come back; but this does not mean that all the battles have been won, or that there will be no more defeats. If the community is uncertain about him, it is just as true that he is uncertain about the community. Inevitably, he wonders what they will think, or worse, what they have been thinking. He does not want to make himself a bore by dwelling on the problem, but he does not want to ignore it as though it never happened. He recognizes that he still has limitations, yet he does not want to be treated as though he might crumble under a hard blow. He is grateful for the concern of well-wishers, but he resists being the object of pity or maudlin sympathy. Ordinarily, he tends to feel somewhat guilty for having succumbed to the distress, whatever its nature, and suspects that people no longer hold him in as high regard as once he hoped they did.

Within these generalities are persons whose task of returning to a way of life which is at once a continuation of the old and a pattern radically new presents the minister with a tremendous opportunity for pastoral care. For if the referral experience will ultimately eventuate in a successful restoration of the parishioner, much will depend on the reestablishment of positive relationships. Here, as elsewhere, the minister is faced with dual responsibilities. On the one hand, he stands with the parishioner as he makes his way back into the community, and on the other he stands with the community as it wrestles with its own feelings about the returned person. Only as these two aspects of pastoral concern are kept in focus is there a good possibility that the restoration will in fact be accomplished.

In regard to the pastor's relationship to the parishioner, the way is made easier if during the referral it was clear that his concern was for restoration—however it would come. Since we have already discussed this process in an earlier chapter, there is no necessity to repeat it here. The essence is that the referral was accomplished without the parishioner feeling rejection by the pastor, and without the pastor feeling threatened that he could not personally provide the help that was needed. Such a relationship throughout the time of distress enables both the pastor and the parishioner to face honestly every aspect of the situation and find genuine encouragement in progress, however slight, since they know the direction in which they are moving and the distance they have already come.

Just as the pastor was involved in the life of the parishioner through the general program of the congregation prior to the time of crisis, so he enjoys the same privilege and opportunity following the intensive care and therapy. Once again he can take the initiative in calling from time to time, in helping to bear part of the burden of discouragement and frustration, and in facilitating the growing capacity of the parishioner to deal constructively with the inevitable tensions which will be encountered along the way. In performing this ministry, he is careful on the one hand to stand with the parishioner when the going is hard but at the same time to avoid any attempt to take over his life and thus prevent the necessary movement toward mature responsibility. The tension between these two is fairly simple to describe, but not always easy to maintain.

In the following excerpt, it is possible to see something of the minister's continued relationship to a parishioner following the time of crisis. The parishioner is the alcoholic described in Chapters One and Three. It will be recalled that the particular binge which led to his referral to AA had lasted about three weeks. As would be expected, his relationships in business, church, and community had been deteriorating badly over a period of time. As a consequence of his association with the members of AA, he began a gradual reconstruction of his life. Painfully he faced up to the fact that he had hurt many people; and even more painfully he set about to make restitution and amends, except where to do so would cause even more distress. As would be expected, he met with both success and failure. Some of those he approached rebuffed him, giving vent to some of the hostility which he had engendered over the years. Many more responded in a kind of bewildered disbelief as he came this time to ask only for forgiveness, rather than a loan or a favor as so often before. And, of course, many had no opportunity to understand something of the struggle through which he had passed and was passing but were glad that on the surface, at least, things seemed to be better with him.

At the time of this excerpt, the pastor had called to invite him to lunch. After coffee, they had a few minutes free from interruption before returning to their offices.

1. *Minister:* How's it going, Norman? I've thought about you a lot recently, even though our paths haven't crossed much.

2. *Norman:* Just no comparison with the old days. Oh, I hit some rough spots, but it's wonderful to be able to thank the good Lord each night that I haven't had a drink that day.

3. *Minister:* I'm real glad to hear it. I imagine that it hasn't all been rosy, but it's good to know that the general direction is up.

4. *Norman:* Yeah. You know, it's a funny thing your calling me to have lunch with you. I've been wanting to talk with you about something, but somehow didn't know how to start.

5. *Minister:* Well, I'm in no big hurry right now if this seems like a good time to you.

6. *Norman:* It's about coming to your church. I used to go to church when I was a kid, but then I went away to college, and I don't know. . . . Then Elsie and I got married, and we moved here and the children came along, and then I got to drinking as you know, and . . . well, we didn't think much about the Church. Elsie used to say we ought to go, but I'd just get mad and yell at her. I don't know . . .

7. *Minister:* I suppose the Church was the last thing you wanted to have anything to do with in those days.

8. *Norman:* Boy, that's the truth! But it's not like that now. You've got something I need real bad, but . . . well, to tell you the truth, I sort of hesitate to come. Most of those people know I was a pretty bad drunk, and I don't know what they'll think if I show up at church. And then . . . well, I don't know much about the Bible or anything, and I'd sure hate for them to ask me something or call on me for something . . . I'd just die. . . .

There are several temptations which confront the pastor at this point. Primarily, he is tempted to defend the congregation by trying to reassure this parishioner that certainly the people in his church will welcome him whenever he comes. Obviously, such is not the case. Inevitably, there will be those who respond negatively to a Prodigal returning to the Father's house. At a more subtle level, he is tempted to minimize the difficulties in order to add one more member to his rolls. In this vein he would not attempt to assure that there would be no one who would look askance at Norman's coming, but he would note that such persons are in the minority; and besides, their attitude is not representative of the Church as a whole. However accurate this assessment of the congregation might be, it tends to obscure the fact that the returning Prodigal must be ready to face realistically the possible rejection of members of the congregation—and that any obscuring of this potentiality leads to a crisis more destructive than that occasioned by an honest facing of that which is. From a different perspective, the pastor is tempted to avoid providing the help actually needed in the mistaken notion that the parishioner needs to walk the road alone. In such a circumstance, he fails to recognize the basic difference between creative help and destructive paternalism.

In the continuing interview, the pastor did not completely escape these temptations, but his relationship to the parishioner was essentially constructive.

9. *Minister:* So that you're real hesitant to come on over there, afraid of what they might do to you. . . .

10. *Norman:* Yeah. Like I say, if they called on me, I'd sure strike out. 'Course, I guess I'm just borrowing trouble, but I'd hate to get over there and . . .

11. *Minister:* May not happen, but the fact that it might really bugs you.

12. *Norman:* Yeah. Yet I know I ought to go. In the old days I used to stay away from things that might hurt. But this is different.

13. *Minister:* Are you saying that coming to church really means something, and you don't want to mess it up.

14. *Norman:* Yeah. (pause) But you know, if I do my part, that's all I can manage. Maybe some of those guys in church are having a rough time, too.

15. *Minister:* Well, I'm sure they are. If I hear you right, you're wondering whether you may be taking what they think too seriously.

16. *Norman:* Could be. Even so, it's not a picnic to think of going up there, and, well . . .

17. *Minister:* So you'd probably jump no matter what they said or did, since you feel sort of gun-shy already.

18. *Norman:* Yeah. (long pause) Gosh, Reverend, it's not easy just to walk in church after all these years.

19. *Minister:* So you'd like to come, but just aren't sure you could make it.

20. *Norman:* Yeah. You think they'd let me in church knowing what I've done.

21. *Minister:* Norman, I can give you the straight word on that, at least as far as the Session goes. They are much more interested in who you are *now* than in what you've done. In that sense, they would want to know how much you have grown in this situation, rather than where you came from. I guess this is really a hard thing to hear in the sense that you have never found it to be true.

22. *Norman:* Yeah, And yet I'd surely like for it to be true. I think you know what I mean. . . .

23. *Minister:* Well, I'm not real sure. Maybe that you wish what I said was true, but it's sort of hard to believe.

24. *Norman:* Yeah. And that if somebody started looking at me like "Well, what's this drunk doing in church?" I'd not get all resentful and go out and get plastered. . . .

25. *Minister:* I see what you mean. Coming up there'd really be running a risk, and you aren't sure how you'd do. . . .

26. *Norman:* That's right. I've come a long way, and I really don't want to blow it now.

Despite the fact that certain of the minister's responses could have been improved, he managed to maintain a fairly good balance between affirmation of the situation, as he saw it, and acceptance of the parishioner's point of view. As it turned out, Norman did come to church with his wife and children, and at the time of the minister's making this report had remained a faithful member of the congregation. When the expected rebuffs came, he was able to meet them in terms of their realistic meaning with the continued help of the minister. While this account is not presented as a success story, as if to say that all such situations will turn out positively if only certain strategies are observed, it does illustrate that which is possible in the restoration of the parishioner to the community.

The other half of the pastor's responsibility concerns his relationship to the congregation. As we have already noted, the varied feelings represent unresolved areas in their own lives and thus present genuine opportunities for pastoral care and personal growth. It is quite naive to expect that an entire congregation will or should be able to relate positively to a returning Prodigal. Such a notion tends to assume that the congregation is composed of mature individuals who have the ability and the resources to relate constructively to those who turn to them for help. To be sure, this is happily true for some in the congregation, but it is certainly not true for all. Ordinarily, the congregation is composed of those who, like Norman, come together because of their need rather than because of their resources. This does not mean that they have nothing to give, for such is not the case. It does mean that a kind of unreflective notion of a congregation as being supposedly well established in the faith fails to take into account the varying stages of growth which are part and parcel of each member of any such group.

The pastor may become irritated when members of his congregation fail to respond redemptively to the Normans who make tentative and hesitant advances toward them. If he does, he bids fair to lose an opportunity to help either Norman or the people in his church.

He can, of course, wish that his people were more mature in their faith, so that they could relate more positively to the Normans who come. But he will not overlook the opportunity which this kind of encounter evokes. Just as he was able to sit down with Norman and help work through his own uncertainties regarding coming to church, so is it possible that he can sit down with members of the congregation to help them wrestle with their feelings of rejection toward the Normans. While it is true that the Elder Brother may never become reconciled to the genuine welcome accorded the Prodigal, the pastor's responsibility is to go out to meet him with the same warmth and forgiveness that he showed for the Younger Son so that at least there is the realistic opportunity that he, too, may grow in the experience.

It should not be assumed, of course, that the minister's relationship to the congregation on the occasion of the Prodigal's return is simply one to one. Just as there is a place for study groups, as indicated in the previous section, so there is need for a corporate awareness of the redemptive nature of the Church. If it is impossible to expect that the entire congregation can readily speak the word of welcome to the returning member, it is certainly appropriate to cultivate smaller groups within the congregation which can perform this kind of function. Forms will naturally vary from situation to situation. Nevertheless, the idea behind the notion of a "House Church" or a "Prayer Group" suggests the sort of structure which can manifest the healing nature of the congregation. And the unexpected benefit of such strategies is the fact that in ministering to the Prodigals, whatever the particular distress, members of such groups discover that they tend to receive far more than they give. The fact is that, just as the account of the scene in Matthew 25 records, those who give themselves in the service of others find that they have met the Lord.

Ministry Continues

In a basic sense, there is no way to conclude a book on any aspect of pastoral care as though a formula had been devised which could assure success whatever happened. Troubles have a way of resolving themselves or emerging into new forms even more destructive than before. However desirable it might seem to be able to get everything settled so that the persons might live happily ever after, the fact is that life simply does not move in that channel. Just as every event has countless antecedents, so the eventualities are infinite.

What actually happens when all goes well is that the person becomes able to cope with the variety of circumstances with which he has to strive, without being overwhelmed or thwarted in his onward course. It is a truism that most problems of life are actually insoluble. This does not mean that certain adjustments cannot be made; it does mean that basically the resolution is in the person rather than in the situation. Years ago St. Paul put the matter succinctly. "I am able," he said, "to meet any situation through Christ who gives me strength." (Philippians 4:13, paraphrase).

The secret of success, therefore, lies not so much in a rearrangement of circumstance as in a process whereby the person is strengthened to deal with that which is part and parcel of his life. It is in this sense that therapy seeks to enable the individual to cope with life in all its complexities, recognizing that there is no way he can be spared the adversities and frustrations which are inevitable in the normal course of events. The essence of therapy, therefore, is the momentary lifting of the burden which is crushing the life out of the person and the making available of resources upon which he can draw, so that he may take up the load again with some prospect of success.

So it is that the minister welcomes the varieties of skills which have been developed through the years for lightening the burden and making it possible for the person to receive strength. Seen in this holistic fashion, all the helping professions assume a significant role in the healing of the ills of life. It is inevitable that not each one will define itself in terms of the ultimate questions of life; indeed, most would consider such a definition presumptuous on its face. It is also inevitable that some will assume more than is in fact possible within the scope of their own definition and, thus, tend to heal too lightly the distress of the people.

In the final analysis, neither of these eventualities need disturb the minister whose concern is the welfare of his parishioners. Just as he will not attempt to require a theological formula from those whose self-imposed limits enable them to deal effectively with one aspect of life, so he will not refuse the constructive assistance of those who claim more than is appropriate. In drawing on the genuine resources of the helping professions, he does not relinquish the ministry of wholeness which is able to set each aspect in a broader context.

Never does he forget that his ministry is fashioned according to the pattern of One who rebuked the disciples when they attempted to forbid help by those who did not follow after them. It is in this sense that the minister is able to join hands with all sorts and varieties of men whose intention is the alleviation of human suffering. To be sure he does not approach their work uncritically nor fall prey to every voice that is raised offering help. He recognizes that there are always those who traffic in trouble and exploit those who are harassed by situations which bid fair to overwhelm them. At the same time, he is able to make common cause with those who give themselves to the task of helping others even when there are theoretical issues as yet unresolved. Whatever the proximate or ultimate goals of his colleagues in the helping professions, he is able to keep clearly in mind that there will be no real resolution of distress until the person is rightly related to himself, to his fellows, and to God. Thus it is that the minister has no apprehension when help seems to come from unlikely sources. In the final analysis, he is convinced that all true help comes from Him whose purpose was "that they might have life, and that they might have it more abundantly." (John 10:10 K.J.V.)

Index